DOLLHOUSE
DOLLS

DOLLHOUSE

JOANN McCRACKEN

Photographs by SHERMAN HOWE, Jr.

DOLLS

CHILTON BOOK COMPANY

RADNOR, PENNSYLVANIA

Published in Radnor, Pennsylvania, by Chilton Book Company
and simultaneously in Don Mills, Ontario, Canada,
by Nelson Canada Limited

Library of Congress Catalog Card No. 80-960
      ISBN 0-8019-6864-X *hardcover*
      ISBN 0-8019-6865-8 *paperback*

Designed by William E. Lickfield

Manufactured in the United States of America

All dollhouses by *Real Good Toys*

3 4 5 6 7 8 9   9 8 7 6 5 4 3 2 1

To *Real Good Toys*
Montpelier, Vermont
John Javna, proprietor

Contents

SECTION II • DOLL BUILDING

Foreword

The special, winsome quality of Joann McCracken's dolls was evident in the first one I saw, some years ago. Since then, I've seen her dolls in many places, including the Atlanta Toy Museum. They adorn handmade dollhouses and miniature room sets across the country and are so appropriate in costume and facial expression that they seem, indeed, to be tiny replicas of people we know.

Joann's humor is present in her dolls: Santa bubbling over with good cheer, Mrs. Santa a bit harassed on Christmas Eve, the stuffy but genial Victorian gentleman, the flustered shopkeeper, and fussy little old ladies with their shopping bags. Joann's dolls will captivate you, and DOLLHOUSE DOLLS will teach you all the skills for making dolls that will be uniquely yours.

Jean Schramm
The Enchanted Dollhouse

Preface

The notion of dollmaking conjures up fantasies of Santa's elves, Geppetto and Pinnochio, and the "March of the Wooden Soldiers." There is a little of that creative magic in all of us. When you make a doll, you give it part of yourself. You put the personality into the character of the doll; you give it the feeling, the flair—the identity.

You will discover and use talents in making dolls that you did not know you had. Every crafts technique can be used in dollmaking—painting, sculpture, needlework, ceramics, weaving and more. Even in the earliest stages of your work, a sophisticated, finished doll can be made by combining these techniques. And the more you work, the more accomplished your dolls will be.

Very beautiful dolls can be made by a beginner if you remember to be patient. Don't try to hurry the processes and—best of all—remember that there is nothing that cannot be fixed or done over. Armed with the knowledge that failure is impossible—unless you give up—you *can* be a dollmaker!

Acknowledgments

My appreciation is extended to Lori Bodger for advice and help in preparing this book; to Elizabeth Falk and Patty Glikbarg for sharing their energy and exercising patience; to Lois Jackson for all the interesting bits of information that bring life to the history of costumes; to Natalie Cloud for taking care of all the *Doll People* while I was busy writing; to Claire Javna for providing practical advice and moral support. Special thanks to Sophie Hawkins, a veteran dollmaker, for teaching me so much about dolls.

Section 1

DIME-STORE
DOLLS

$\mathcal{C}hapter$ **1** **Making Your First Doll**

This project has been specially selected for the beginner, although a seasoned dollmaker can incorporate many of these ideas into an already established style. You will start with an inexpensive, plastic, dime-store doll, and turn it into an elegant, handmade doll by altering the body and using a special process to paint it. You will also clothe the doll using very simple patterns, then add the details that make any costuming job *look* complicated. When you are finished, you will find it hard to believe that such a beautiful doll was so easy to create. The transformation is—like magic!

Tools and Materials

Large scissors or a small-toothed saw. You probably already have these, but if not, any hardware store carries coping saws or hacksaw blades with handles.

Wire cutters. Ordinary pliers often have wire cutters built in.

Sandpaper—#220. This is a very fine grade of sandpaper

1-1 "Before" and "after" dime-store dolls.

available at hardware stores, building suppliers, hobby, craft or art supply stores.

Thermostat wire—18/3. This wire can be bought by the foot at any electrical supply store. You need about a foot for this project, but buy a little extra—it's very inexpensive.

Contact cement or rubber cement.

Gesso. Ask for acrylic, prepared gesso (pronounced jess-ō) at any art supply store.

Acrylic paints. Buy small tubes of these colors: cadmium red medium, black, white, yellow ochre, and burnt umber.

Brushes. Four small sizes will do the job: #5, #3, #2, and #00.

Acrylic spray. Buy the *best* quality clear acrylic at your art supply store. The discount brands simply do an inferior job.

White cloth tape. This is often called adhesive tape.

Rouge. A small tin or cake of dry powdered rouge.

Cotton swabs.

Container for water. Both gesso and acrylic paints are water-soluble and require a readily available water source.

Clean damp sponge. Any sponge will work as long as it is clean; small pieces are sometimes easier to use.

Rags. Old undershirts are my favorite, but any absorbent material, even paper towels, will work.

Magnifying glass. This can be helpful when working on the facial features.

High intensity lamp. Daylight is best, but if you can't work by a window, use a bright light source.

Choosing the Right Doll

The type of doll needed for this project is commonly found in dime stores. It can be either hard or soft plastic; and the arms and legs can be either stationary or movable. Try to buy dolls with molded hair and painted-on eyes: these are easier for beginners to work with.

This project can be done in any scale, but one-inch-equals-one-foot is the most common dollhouse scale. Dolls should be about 5 to 5½ inches for a woman and 6 inches for a man. If you do find it difficult to locate the right size doll, check Sources of Supply in the back of this book. It is a good idea to buy two or more dolls, as they are very inexpensive. A back-up supply is good insurance; and most likely, after you have done one you will want to do another.

The basic form of these plastic dolls is every bit as good as those made of finer materials. I wouldn't be a bit surprised if some of the molds that made the dime-store dolls came from very old dolls in the first place. The doll in Fig. 1-3 looks very much like one of the early china dolls.

1-2 Commonly available dime-store dolls.

Body Alterations

The first step in our doll-making is alterations to the body. Dime-store dolls are usually somewhat out of proportion, so you will have to either shorten or lengthen the arms and legs.

You accomplish these changes by removing the limbs and reattaching them with 18/3 thermostat wire. By using this heavy flexible wire you do two things at once: the limbs become the correct length, and they become bendable, a desirable quality for more life-like dolls.

Chapter 5 contains a complete discussion of proportion, including several illustrations to help you size your doll. Keep this rule in mind: a person's height is equal to the distance from fingertip to fingertip with arms outstretched.

The so-called "fashion" dolls have legs that are too long; they will have to be shortened. Sometimes the legs on a child doll can be lengthened to make an adult. Almost all inexpensive plastic dolls have arms that are too short.

Remember that no two people have the exact same measurements; your dolls can differ in similar ways. Measure members of your family to get a sampling of various sizes, and then translate these into dollhouse scale.

Because of the inter-relationship of the dimensions of the arms and legs, you should decide on these dimensions before you start cutting your doll apart.

Arms

To alter the arms, you must first remove them. Usually you can just unsnap them or pull them out and snip the rubber band. If the shoulders are stationary, start cutting or sawing (Fig. 1-3). Scissors will work on pliable plastic; on brittle material, you will have to saw, very gently.

After the arms have been removed from the body, cut through each arm about halfway between the wrist and elbow. Keep the hands with wrists attached and throw the upper arm away.

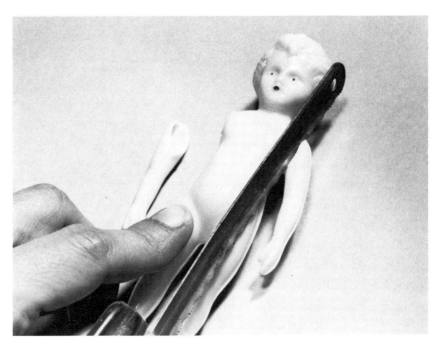

1-3 Gently remove the doll's arms with the blade of a small saw.

To extend the length of the arms, you will need a piece of 18/3 thermostat wire with casing. Because this wire is durable, firm and flexible, it makes the perfect wire armature for miniature dollmaking.

One continuous piece of wire is used for both arms. To determine the length of this wire, lay your doll down on a ruler, positioning the arm pieces the proper distance apart (Fig. 1-4). Measure the space between the arms, and add a little extra at each end to be inserted into the arms. (Remember how much extra you add, so that you insert the wire to the proper point.) If the arms are solid, do not add this extra wire.

Now you attach *one* of the arm pieces to the wire. Coat the wire end and end of the forearm with contact cement. If the arm is solid, these ends will butt up against each other. If the arm is hollow, the wire is inserted into the arm to the proper point.

For this connection you will have to depend heavily on the adhesive tape for strength. After you have peeled off the excess glue, wind the forearm with tape. Wind tape around

1-4 Measure arms for correct length.

the arm, around the connection and around the wire (Fig. 1-5). If the connection doesn't seem strong enough, go over it again with another piece of tape, but be careful that you don't make a bulge, or your doll's arms will look like they belong to Popeye.

Poke the other end of the wire through the armholes of the doll's body. Now is the time to check to make sure you have the right or left hand on the correct side of the body. Attach the other hand to the other end of the wire in the same way, making sure both hands have the thumbs up.

Center the wire so that both arms are the same length. Wrap cloth tape in a figure-eight, shoulder to shoulder (Fig. 1-6 and 1-7). Make sure that the arms are secure but not bulky.

Legs

There are two ways to change the length of your doll's legs. The first is used if you are shortening the legs, and if it is

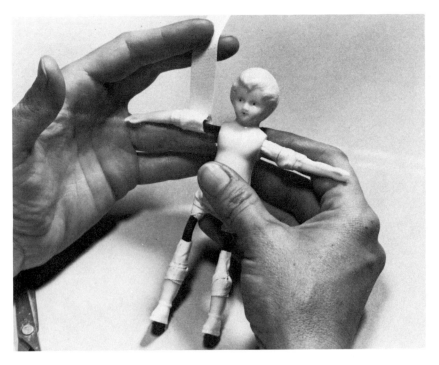

1-5 Wrapping cloth tape around arm.

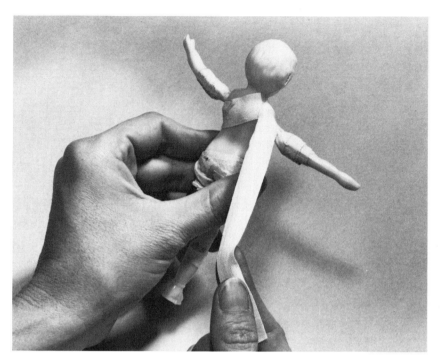

1-6 Beginning figure-eight around shoulders.

1-7 Finishing figure-eight around shoulders.

not important for them to bend. Decide how much they need to be shortened, and cut out a piece this size centered over the knee. The lower leg is then reattached directly to the thigh with contact cement. Tape the connection to give it strength.

If you are lengthening the legs or if it is important to have bendable knees, the alterations are done with wire as the arms were. Cut off the legs slightly below the hips, rather than right at the hips. Then cut through the legs about halfway between knee and ankle. The upper leg can be discarded.

Measure the wires, adding extra to be inserted into the hips and the feet. Attach the feet to the wires, and then the wires to the hips, as you did with the arms. Use adhesive tape to give the connections strength. (Make sure the feet are on the correct side—the big toes to the inside.) Wrap a figure-eight around the hips if necessary.

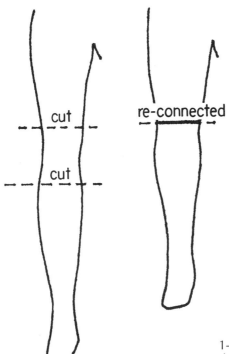

cut

cut

re-connected

1-8 "Before" and "after" shortening doll's leg.

Gesso is a wonderful material that has been used for centuries by artists for preparing canvas for painting, and by craftsmen for decorating furniture and picture frames.

The Gesso Application

When wet, the acrylic, prepared gesso that you will use is a white, thick material that has the consistency of yogurt. The fact that it is water soluble makes it easy to use and quick to clean up. Among other ingredients, gesso contains a large percentage of glue, so that it adheres well to almost any surface.

When you paint the gesso on your doll, layers will build up on the plastic, but the original form of the doll will show through. Later this form will serve as a guide for painting hair, facial features and shoes. When thoroughly dry, gesso has a very hard, insoluble finish which can be sanded or carved. It looks very much like plaster or unglazed porcelain.

Surface Preparation

Before you start applying the gesso, the plastic surface of the doll's body must be prepared. Using a small piece of #220 sandpaper, rub very gently, as if you were giving a new baby a bath. Do not apply pressure or scrub. You merely want to raise a little "tooth," in other words, remove the smoothness so that the gesso has something to cling to. Start with the body of the doll, then sand the legs and feet.

If your doll came with hair glued on, it should be removed. It is usually easier for beginners to use dolls with molded hair. When you come to the head, you can use a little more pressure to try to remove the seam line that often appears on inexpensive dolls. Do little sanding on the face—very, very lightly on the cheeks and forehead, but do not disturb the eyes, nose and mouth.

Applying the Gesso

Now paint the surface of the doll with gesso. Start with your #2 brush. You can get the feel of working with gesso by practicing your stroke on the back of the doll's body, or any other part that will not show after the doll is clothed. The gesso will stick to the wire and the adhesive tape, but it is only necessary to apply it to parts of the doll that will be exposed later.

Use light, even strokes. The first coat should be thin enough to allow the color of the plastic to show through faintly. If you find that you are getting a streaky, bumpy effect, you are using too much gesso on your brush.

It is sometimes helpful to use another dry brush to brush it to a smooth surface. Gesso dries very quickly, so be sure to smooth it out as you go.

Do not let your brushes dry with gesso on them. Since it is water soluble, you should keep a glass of water on your worktable and clean your brushes from time to time. Don't be too concerned if some of the streaks do dry, because you will be applying three more layers. In the end, if you still don't have an even surface, the gesso can be sanded smooth.

When you have finished the back, paint the front of the body. Then work your way down the legs and paint the feet. While this is drying a bit, gesso the hands.

Complete the first coat by working up to the head, putting an extra heavy coat on the hair. Brush in the same direction as the grooves of molded hair. This is the time to take advantage of the thick texture of the gesso. You can use that streaky effect that you had been previously trying to avoid, to give the impression of waves or curls on your doll's head. Figure 1-9 shows three different hair treatments. The doll on the left had short vinyl hair which was thoroughly saturated with gesso; it will take several days to dry. The middle doll had molded hair that was accented by the gesso. The doll on the right is bald; it can be left this way with a head covering, or have fiber hair added, as discussed in Chapter 4.

The part of the doll with which you must be most careful is the face. On a dollhouse doll, you are working on such a tiny scale that a small blob of gesso next to the nose could cause an extra nose. As you apply gesso to the face use a tiny #0 brush and be sure to have your dry brush handy; the gesso tends to collect under the nose and around the eyes and mouth.

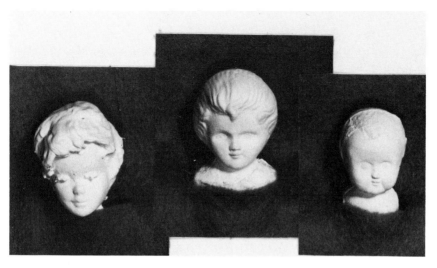

1-9 Three different hair treatments.

If your doll has eyes that open and close, you can decide which way to leave them before applying the gesso. However, if the eyelashes are molded in, the face will look better if the eyes are left open.

The second coat, in which you repeat the entire process, can be done after two hours of drying time. Remember to go easy on the face. With this coat, you should not be able to see the color showing through, but don't make it so thick that you lose the facial features.

Sometimes these dolls come with shoes molded to the feet. Others come with the most ugly little plastic shoes imaginable. Don't throw them away! Those see-through, char-treuse sandals can come through looking like a pair of the very finest high-button shoes of the late 1800's.

Remove the shoes, and after two coats of gesso have been applied to the feet, put them back on. They probably will not fit easily, but do the best you can to get them firmly in place. Now dunk the whole foot, shoe and all, into your gesso pot. Remove the foot slowly, allowing the excess to drip back into the pot.

Meanwhile, gently brush up the leg with your #2 flat brush to smooth the surface to blend with the rest of the leg coating. On the shoes, the only place to try to remove the excess gesso is the sole; the bottom of the shoe should be flat. Lightly brush the top of the shoe so the shape of the shoe isn't completely lost. Let the gesso remain in the spaces between the foot and the shoe. You may have to repeat the dunking process to make sure that foot and shoe become one solid unit. The glue in the gesso will harden and keep the shoe in place after it has dried completely.

Don't be fooled by the fact that gesso dries superficially in a matter of minutes. It takes about 12 hours for it to become thoroughly dry. Allow the first two coats to become completely dry and hard.

An inexpensive doll usually has a seam that runs down the sides and around the top of the head. This is the place where the molded pieces meet. In making fine china dolls this seam is shaved before the piece is fired. On your doll, the seam will probably be sticking up, making a ridge around the doll, dividing the front and back halves. With an X-acto or other sharp knife, carefully shave the gesso ridge which covers

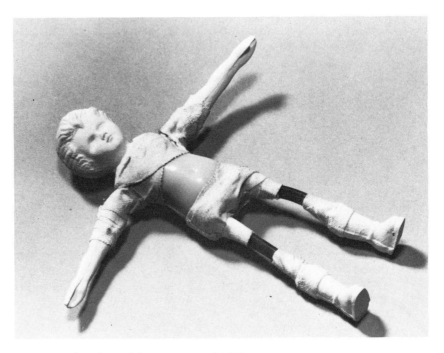

1-10 Face, hands and feet are coated with gesso.

the plastic seam, and make the surface level. You may have to cut through some of the plastic seam in the places where the ridge is very high.

Now paint the whole doll, except the face, with two more coats of gesso, and let it dry. With the fourth and final coat of gesso, the doll should have a smooth, hard surface all over, and will have lost its cheap, dime-store appearance.

Final Touches

The time has come to paint your doll. This step is fun, because the changes are so dramatic. If this is your first time with tiny brush in hand, don't panic. There is nothing you can do that cannot be done over. Just follow along step-by-step. We will start on the easiest part—the legs—and work our way up. Before you know it the eyelashes will be in place.

Acrylic paint is foolproof! It is water soluble—easy to clean up and easy to mix to a workable consistency by simply adding water. If you should make a little mistake (all mistakes are little when working in miniature), you can whisk it away with a clean damp sponge, without disturbing the dry layer of paint beneath. If your little mistake dries, it can be painted over with one coat. Acrylic paint covers so well that black paint can be covered with white in one or two coats. This paint dries very quickly, so if you need to cover up, it only takes a few minutes until you can start again.

This quick-drying paint also takes only a few minutes to ruin a brush if you forget to wash it immediately after using. Keep a glass of water and a rag handy. When you finish using a brush, pop it into the water. When you need it again, rinse it out, wipe it off, and it's ready.

When you are finished for the day, rinse all the paint out of the brushes. Then rub the bristles on a cake of hand soap, rinse them again under running water, and repeat this process until the water is clear. Shape the damp bristles to a point or flat edge, depending on the type of brush, and let them dry that way. Good brushes are more expensive, but they will last for years with proper care.

Before you start painting your doll, practice on scrap paper or palette paper. Squeeze a small amount of paint on your palette, no more than the toothpaste you would put on your toothbrush. Dip your #5 brush into the water and tap the excess on the side of the glass. The brush should be just damp enough to carry a small amount of water to the paint. Mix the water at the edge of the paint on the palette. You are aiming for a consistency that is thick enough so it isn't runny, but not so thick that you can see brush marks. Experiment with different brush sizes and amounts of water and paint until you have the feeling that the paint is flowing smoothly.

Painting the Body

Start on the doll by painting the legs and feet. Black shoes and stockings are traditional and conveniently easy to paint. Start at the top of the legs and paint down to the feet in nice long, even strokes. You will know right away if your paint is too thick, because your strokes will be short and streaky. If the paint is too thin, that will immediately be apparent, also. The paint will run right down the leg, off the toes and land in your lap! Just add more paint or more water until the mixture is easy to control.

When the legs and feet are dry, in about five minutes, paint the hands and arms with fleshtone. If you have had some experience with acrylic paint, you may wish to mix your own skin color. The basic formula for mixing fleshtone is 90 percent white, 5 percent cadmium red (med.), and 5 percent yellow ochre. Most skin colors are variations on this formula. Start with a very small amount of white. Add much smaller quantities of cadmium red and yellow ochre in equal amounts until the color looks like fleshtone. (Unused paint mixture can be stored in a plastic bag and used for touchups.) Another alternative is "china doll" white. If this is the look that you want, use titanium white.

The hands and arms are painted with your #5 brush. But when you start working on the neck and face, switch to the same technique that you used when you were painting the gesso on the face. Use a smaller #3 brush, and have a clean, damp #3 in the other hand so you can quickly smooth over drips and places on the doll's face, eyelids, nose, and lips where paint collects and features lose definition.

When painting the face, you should apply the paint in a much thinner coat than you did on the arms and legs. If the color does not look even, add another coat of paint, after the first layer is dry. Two thin coats of paint are better than one thick one.

Painting the Hair

You are now faced with an important decision—you must choose a color for the hair. The co-ordination of the hair, eyes, and clothing will create an image, which is so important in giving the doll a personality. There is an image which is automatically associated with blue eyes and blonde hair, another image for the lady with raven-colored locks and black, flashing eyes, and yet another for the flaming redhead. Other associations are more subtle and more subconscious—for example, freckles, or green eyes.

As you choose the hair color, look at your doll; think of a person you know, a famous personality, or maybe someone you saw walking down the street. An illustration from an old picturebook for children could be the inspiration that you need to tie the image to the character for your doll.

After you have decided on the image that suits you and your doll, paint the hair color. Follow the lines of the original mold; let your brush follow the grooves and contours that are there. Use your tiny #00 brush for the hairline. If you should go over the line and paint the hair color onto the face, just wait until it dries and cover it up with the Fleshtone. If your doll is bald, Chapter 4 contains complete instructions on adding fiber hair.

Painting the Facial Features

To help in placing the facial features, first draw in the lips, eyebrows and eyelash lines using very pale yellow paint.

Once you have the features sketched in to your satisfaction, you can start filling in the colors. Paint the lips red or pink, depending on the image the doll is to project.

The eyes are probably the most difficult to paint, so have your clean, damp sponge handy. If you are right-handed, you will have more control on the right side of the doll's face. Start on the left side, so that when you paint the right side, you will have the extra amount of control necessary for making the eyes match.

It is sometimes easier to control the brush stroke on the left side of the face by turning the doll upside down and holding the head in your other hand (Fig. 1-11). Then turn the doll right-side-up to work on the right side (Fig. 1-12).

Start by painting the whites of the eyes: paint an almond-shaped area under each eyelash. Wait a few minutes until they dry, then paint the eyelash lines in burnt umber.

When the eyelash lines are dry, paint the eyebrows the same color as the hair. A very thin arched line is good for

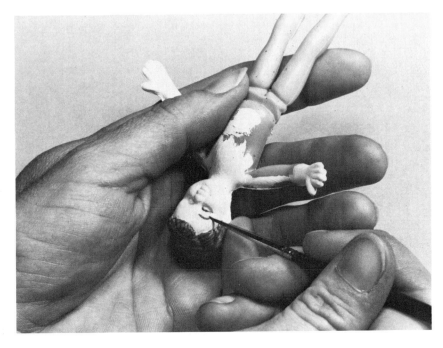

1-11 Holding upside-down to paint left side.

1-12 Holding right-side-up to paint right side.

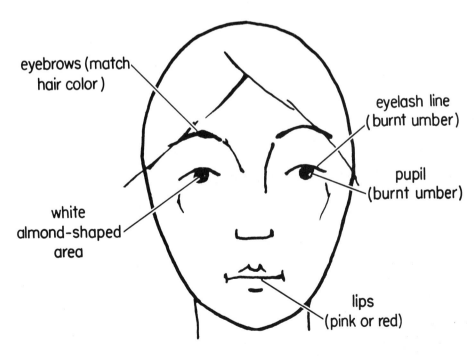

eyebrows (match hair color)

eyelash line (burnt umber)

pupil (burnt umber)

white almond-shaped area

lips (pink or red)

1-13 Painting in facial features.

1-14 Several eyebrow treatments.

ladies. A series of overlapping dots make suitable eyebrows for men. Children's eyebrows are very thin and very short. If the eyebrows are not indicated by the mold, be careful how you place them. If the eyebrows are too high, the doll will look surprised; if they are too low, the doll will look angry.

When the eyebrows are in place and you are satisfied with the expression, paint a tiny dot of burnt umber, which will represent the iris and the pupil. (You may use another eye color on this doll, but wait until the painting is completed on the features. Then go back and paint over the burnt umber dot.) The placement of the pupils is somewhat more difficult than the other features. The real trick is getting the second one to be looking in exactly the same direction as the first. When working at this scale, it is very easy to make the eyes crossed or have one eye trailing off in another direction. It is a good thing that you have an infinite number of chances to do it over until it comes out just right.

1-15 A finished face.

For a final examination, hold the doll at arms length and look at it. Sometimes you can see *more* from *farther* away. You give yourself a fresh perspective. It is a good idea to stop and look at your work from a distance at various stages throughout the development of your doll.

Rosy Cheeks

The final touch that really brings your doll's face to life is giving it rosy cheeks. The change is amazing and this technique is truly necessary to the successful painting of a doll's face. Use powdered rouge, the kind made for people. Rub it on in a circular motion with a cotton swab or the tip of your finger. A female doll should be a little rosier than men or children. To set the rouge and protect the paint, spray lightly with a good quality clear, acrylic spray.

The body of your doll is now finished. You have transformed an ordinary doll into a beautiful personality. Have you thought of a name yet?

Chapter 2 **Simple Clothing**

Now that you have finished your doll's body, it is time to add the clothing to complete the image. As you work on the costume, you can almost see your doll coming to life. You can't wait to add the little bits of lace or tiny buckles that will set everything off.

The patterns and instructions in this chapter are very simple. The finished product, however, will be quite elegant. The patterns provide for the basic clothes, then you decide on the all-important finishing touches that create the character.

If your past experiences with doll's clothing have been frustrating because of all the tiny seams, my method of construction will solve the problem. I have found that by using fabric glue, the clothing is much easier to put together. These costumes are not removable; the pieces are glued onto the body one at a time.

Tools and Materials

Fabric. A lightweight, small print fabric is best.

Scissors. These should be sharp, especially the points, for working on the small pieces.

Fabric glue. There are several types, but I prefer the type that is the same color and consistency as common white glue.

Trim. Narrow lace, ribbon or rickrack, tiny buckles, etc.

Straight pins, needles and thread to match fabric.

Clothes pins. The spring-type pins make excellent clamps when gluing tiny things.

Choosing the Fabric

Choosing the right fabric is not only important to the looks of the doll's clothes but essential to the mechanics of dressmaking in miniature. The cloth cannot be too heavy or too light; the size of the print must be in scale, and the material must suit the character of your doll. Take your doll with you when you go shopping for fabric and drape the corner of the cloth around the doll to get a good idea of how it will look.

Some man-made fabrics will not work with glue; they simply will not stick. So, make sure the fabric has a high percentage of cotton, if not 100 percent. Regular cotton percale is the best material to use for shirts and dresses. Felt is best for men's pants.

Tiny flowered prints or light solids are the easiest to work with for the beginner because if a piece becomes slightly crooked while under construction, it is not as noticeable. Stripes and plaids have to be matched up, and kept in line throughout the process. It really isn't that hard to do, but if you want to ensure success on the first doll, use calico or a pale solid color. Dark solids are at the very bottom of the acceptable list (except for fabrics with nap). Every drop of glue that is the slightest bit out of place shows up as a dark shiny spot and stands out like a sore thumb! Dark solids with nap are fine.

As you become skilled in costuming you will graduate to more difficult types of fabric in order to create special characters. But for your first experience in making miniature clothes with fabric glue, use cotton or felt.

Women's Clothing

If you did not alter the length of your woman doll's legs and you painted them black, you can choose to skip making underwear altogether and have a perfectly good doll, wearing long, black stockings.

If you did have to change the length of the doll's legs, or if you think that she really should have "bloomers," you will want to make either pantaloons or pantalettes.

Pantaloons or Pantalettes

Pantaloons and pantalettes are made of white cotton. Pantaloons reach to the ankle and have much more lace than pantalettes which come only to the knee.

Instructions

1. Measure your doll from just above the waist to the place where you want the bloomers to stop (Fig. 2-1). This is the "length."
2. Cut two pieces of white cotton—3 inches wide by the "length."
3. On *one* of the pieces, draw a line with a ballpoint pen—one and one-half inches long (Fig. 2-2). Start the line in the center of the bottom edge and draw up toward the waistline.
4. Put an even line of glue along the sides of the fabric (outside legs seams) and on either side and around the top of the pen line (the inside leg seams) (Fig.2-3).
5. Place the other piece on top and press the glued areas together firmly; let them dry completely.
6. Cut through both pieces of fabric along the pen line (Fig. 2-4).
7. Turn the bloomers right side out and put them on the doll.
8. Gather the top edge of the bloomers around the waist of your doll and tape in place with adhesive tape (Fig. 2-5).
9. Trim the bottom edges with white lace or eyelet (Fig. 2-6). For pantaloons add more layers of lace to cover the cotton.

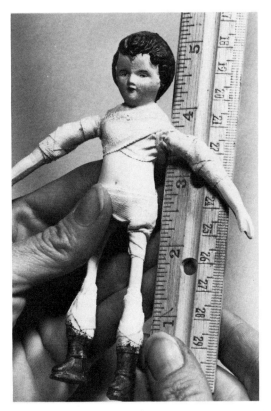

2-1 Measuring for pantaloon length.

2-2 Draw line on pantaloon piece.

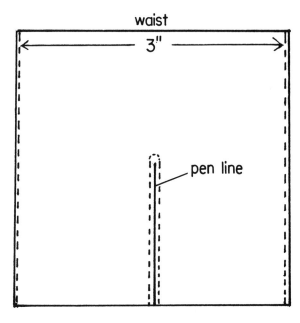

2-3 Apply glue along dotted lines.

2-4 Cut along pen line.

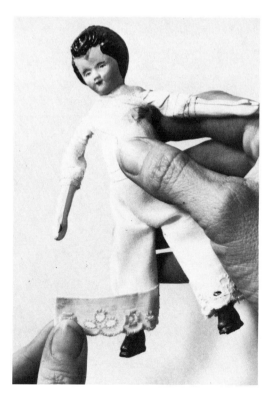

2-5 Tape bloomers to waist.

2-6 Add lace or eyelet trim.

Basic Dress

The pattern for this dress has only two pieces. By following the steps carefully, you will learn the technique for dressing any of the woman dolls from this basic pattern.

Check your pattern pieces to see if they must be altered to fit your doll. Stretch out the arms and hold the doll over the sleeve pattern. If her wrists come to the dotted line which represents the hemmed cuff, the size is right.

Hold the doll over the pattern for the body of the dress (Fig. 2-8). Make her shoulders even with the dotted lines on the shoulders of the pattern. The bottom of her shoes should be even with the dotted line at the bottom of the pattern (hemline). The dress will actually be a little bit shorter when it is on the doll.

The heavy black lines are cutting lines and the dotted lines are seams or hems. Trace these patterns onto a piece of paper and cut them out to use as patterns.

Sleeve Assembly

1. Cut neck opening as shown on pattern. Make sure cuts do not extend past the shoulders.
2. Glue ⅛" hems on one edge and both cuffs as indicated (Fig. 2-9).
3. Use a large pencil or the handle of your X-acto knife (or any cylinder that is larger than your doll's arm) to roll and glue the sleeves (Fig. 2-10). Glue hemmed edge on top of raw edge between "X" and cuff. Let dry completely.
4. Bend both of your doll's arms straight back and slide both sleeves on at the same time (Fig. 2-11).
5. Bend arms back to normal position and secure the flaps in front with glue (Fig. 2-12).

Dress Assembly

1. Glue hems around armholes on both pieces as indicated on pattern pieces (Fig. 2-13).
2. Glue side seams by putting a line of glue along both

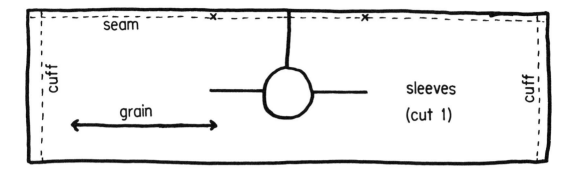

seam

cuff

cuff

grain

sleeves
(cut 1)

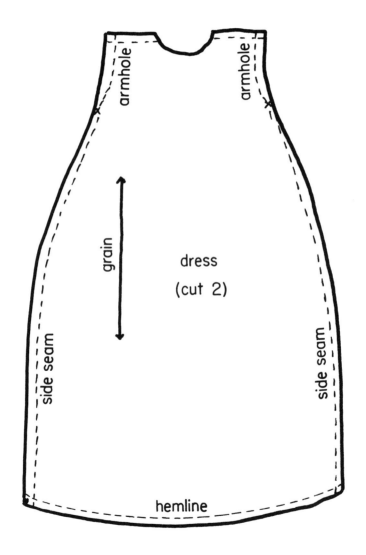

armhole

armhole

grain

dress
(cut 2)

side seam

side seam

hemline

2-7 Pattern for Basic Woman's Dress.

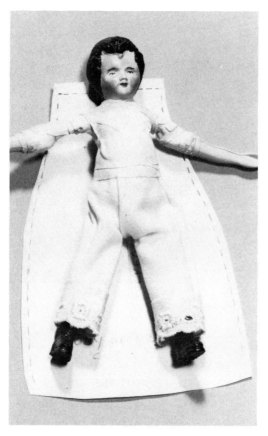

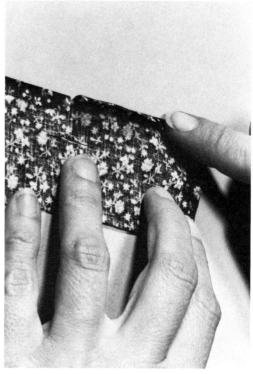

2-9 Glue hem along one side.

2-8 Adjusting pattern to doll.

sides of the *right* side of one of the dress body pieces. Then place both pieces together with right sides facing each other.

3. After the seams have dried completely, turn right side out.

4. Put the doll into the dress feet first. Tie a thread around the waist to see exactly how deep the hem needs to be around the bottom. Check shoulders and under the arms to make sure that you have glued the side seams up high enough.

5. Take the dress off again and glue in the bottom hem.

6. Put the dress back on again, and tie another thread around the waist. Adjust gathers and pleats so that they are even.

2-10 Glue sleeves together.

7. Make a belt out of the same dress material or use a contrasting color in ribbon or trim (Fig. 2-14).
8. Glue the belt in place and secure with straight pins until it is dry.
9. Glue the back shoulder pieces in place (Fig. 2-15).

2-11 Put both sleeves on doll at same time.

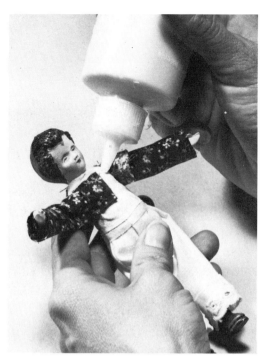

2-12 Glue sleeve flaps to front of doll.

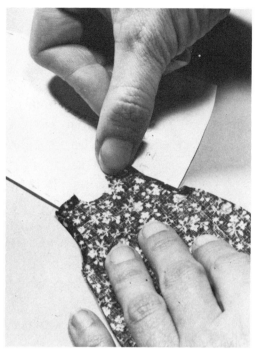

2-13 Glue armhole hems.

2-14 Add belt of same or contrasting fabric.

Take a tuck in the center of the back of the dress and glue it down.

10. Put a little piece of cotton or batting, if necessary, in the front of the top of the dress.

11. Glue a hem across the top of the front shoulder pieces, so that they stop at the top of the shoulder when glued down. Glue around the armholes and across the top of the front of the dress and carefully press into place, working from the outside of the shoulders in toward the neck on both sides (Fig. 2-16).

12. Add a tiny lace collar or a string of seed beads, or make a lovely apron to complete your doll (Fig. 2-17).

Men's Clothing

Dressing a man doll is obviously a little different from dressing a woman, but the basic technique is the same. The shirt goes on first and its assembly is similar to that of the dress, but it's easier because there is no hemline, waistline or bustline to worry about. There are a couple of tricks to fitting the pants, but they are not difficult.

Fitting Patterns

To fit these patterns to your doll, you have to hold your doll over the pattern pieces and make any necessary adjustments. The shirt body will seem very wide. Be sure to allow for tucks and pleats. There is quite a bit of flexibility here—most alterations can be made on the doll.

If you just cannot tell by holding the doll over the pattern piece, cut the patterns out and try them on the doll; you can always trim them down to size. It is reassuring to note that if you trim them down too much, you have only wasted eight square inches of material and you *have* learned something about fitting patterns.

Shirt

Sleeve Assembly

Sleeves are made the same way as for the woman's dress. Check that section for more complete instructions and illustrations.

2-15 Glue down back shoulders, taking tuck in center for proper fit.

2-16 Glue down front shoulders.

2-17 Adding finishing touches.

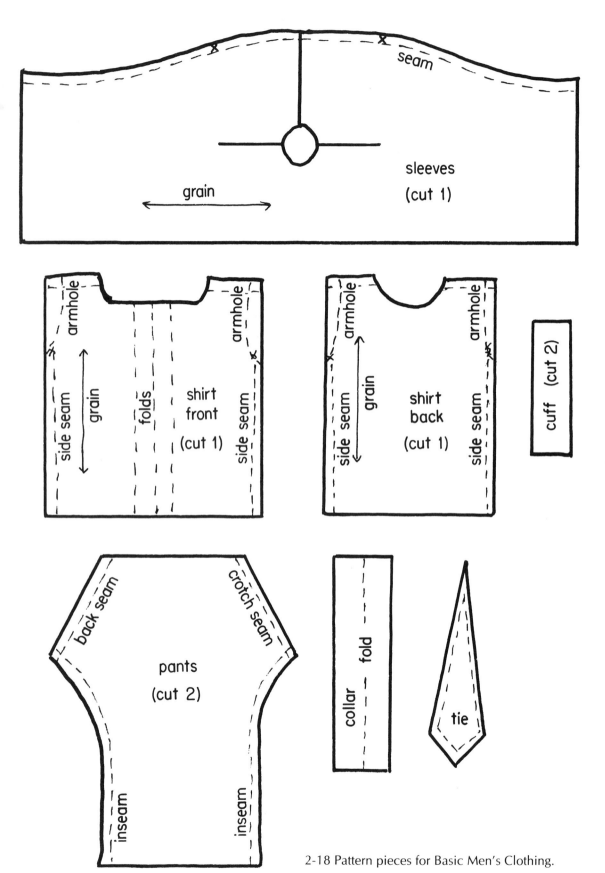

seam

sleeves
(cut 1)

grain

armhole

side seam

grain

folds

shirt
front

(cut 1)

side seam

armhole

armhole

side seam

grain

shirt
back

(cut 1)

side seam

armhole

cuff (cut 2)

back seam

crotch seam

pants
(cut 2)

inseam

inseam

collar — fold

tie

2-18 Pattern pieces for Basic Men's Clothing.

34

1. Glue hem on seam line as indicated; cuffs of sleeves do not need hems
2. Roll sleeve piece around large pencil and glue hems from "X" to cuff over raw edges to form sleeves.
3. Bend your doll's arms straight back and slide both sleeves on.
4. Secure front flaps to the doll's body with glue.

Shirt Body

1. Glue hems on both armholes on the front and back.
2. Glue side seams (right sides together) and turn right side out when the glue is completely dry.

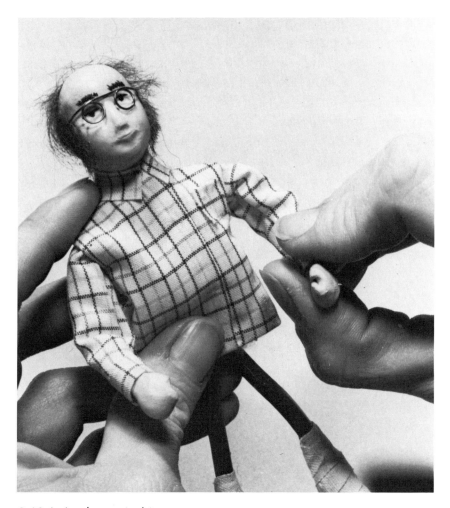

2-19 A simple man's shirt.

3. Slide the doll into the shirt.
4. Glue the back shoulders into place; turn hems on front shoulders and glue to doll.
5. Make a single unpressed pleat at the top center of the back of his neck to fit the shirt to your doll. Glue it in place.
6. Make a similar pleat in the front, but glue it all the way down the front of the shirt. This makes the panel for the buttons.

Collar and Cuffs

The collar and cuff pieces should be cut from double-thickness material, unless you are using a very heavy fabric, such as felt. Spread a thin film of glue on one small piece of material, and press a similar piece on top of it. Make sure there are no bubbles or wrinkles in either piece. Allow glue to dry before cutting out the pieces.

Hold pieces up to the doll to decide on any adjustments that might be necessary. If the shirt is made from fairly heavy material, the cuffs may need to be lengthened to fit. Collar points can be made shorter, longer, or rounded, if desired.

No hems are necessary with these pieces. The collar should be folded in half as indicated on the pattern. Glue all pieces into place; hold with straight pins until glue dries.

Pants

1. Glue the two pants pieces together by gluing the front crotch seam. The pieces can be overlapped (Fig. 2-20) if you are working with felt; if you are working with denim or any material with a raw edge, make a regular glued seam.
2. Wrap the pants around the doll's waist. Make the crotch come to the approximate height; you can fold it under to make a more accurate estimation. If the waistline seems too high you can trim it off or hem it later. Now your main concern is the placement of the crotch.

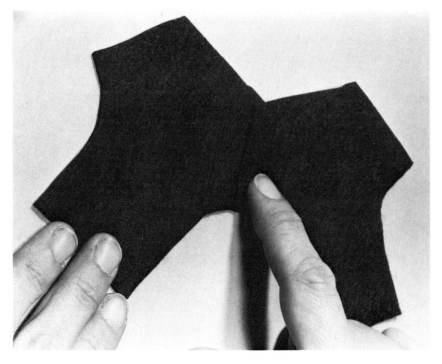

2-20 Gluing front crotch seam.

3. Glue the back seam to make the pants fit snugly around the waist (Fig. 2-21).
4. Glue the inside leg seams in place (Fig. 2-22). Start at the ankle and work your way up each leg until the seams meet and connect at the crotch. The front should overlap the back.

Accessories

You can add a belt made from vinyl or suede cloth or real leather scraps (but use glove leather to stay in scale). The buckle can be a tiny silver or gold button or a tiny buckle from an old watchband. Tiny buckles can also be bought at a jewelry repair shop.

Suspenders can be made from various types of tiny trim. Indian beads can be glued down the shirt front for buttons. You can make a little pocket from matching shirt material, using a scrap that is about the size of your thumbnail. Cuff

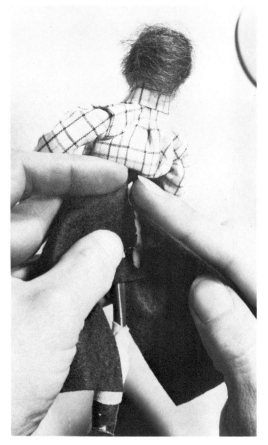

2-21 Gluing back seam of pants.

2-22 Gluing inside leg seams.

2-23 Finished male doll.

links can be made from gold Indian beads sewn or glued in place. You can make a bow-tie, but make it tiny or it will look clownish.

To make a necktie, cut the pattern from a suitable fabric and glue hems in all sides. Loop the top around to look like a knot and glue in place.

Children's Clothing

Children's clothing is basically just smaller versions of the adult clothing you have already made. It is the accessories that create the younger image. Patterns for children will probably have to be adjusted, since no two dolls will be exactly the same age and size. These pattern pieces are intended to fit dolls approximately 3½ to 4 inches tall.

Little Girl

The steps for cutting the patterns and assembling them for a little girl's dress are exactly the same as those for a woman doll. I have added patterns for an apron and a sun bonnet. If you wish, you may omit these extras and add some ideas of your own!

Little Boy

To dress the boy, cut your patterns and follow the assembly steps as you did for the father's shirt and pants. Only the assembly of the shirt front is different for the little boy. The two halves of the shirt front overlap in front along the button panel. Boys' shirts overlap left over right, so hem the left half of the shirt front. Glue the left half on top of the right, and add buttons if you wish.

If you want to make overalls, cut the bib and glue into place. The bottom of the bib is tucked inside the pants. Cross the straps in back, tuck them in and secure with glue.

You can add other accessories to your boy, like patches on the knees and pockets in the back. If you want to add some mischief, make a little slingshot out of a round toothpick and some thread and put it in his back pocket. For a very small boy, make a little boat or a "ducky" out of felt and glue it to the front of his bib.

Baby in Bunting

The patterns and instructions for the baby are the easiest of all and the sweetest. Use felt because it's a perfect miniature translation of the woolly blanket material usually used for buntings. Felt is also the most agreeable fabric to use for this type of costume.

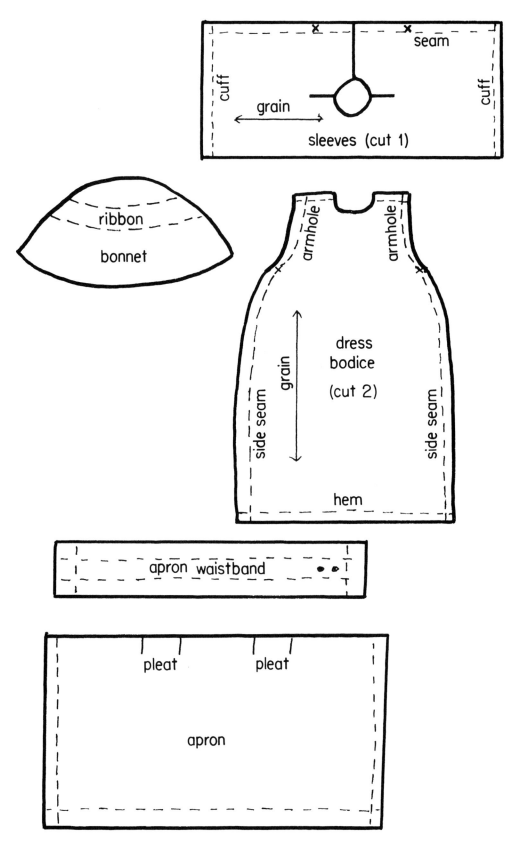

2-24 Pattern pieces for little girl.

2-25 Little girl and boy dolls.

Baby blue or pink are traditional; and since stereotyping is part of creating an illusion, using baby colors is usually a good idea. However, do not feel you are obligated to use only those colors. Baby dolls vary so much in size that several adjustments may have to be made in the pattern size.

Pattern Adjustments

1. Measure the baby from shoulders to toes. Follow the curves in the back and legs with your measuring tape and then add ¼ inch. This will be the length of your bunting pattern piece. Add or subtract fabric at the bottom of the pattern piece.
2. The width of the bunting piece may also need adjustment. The doll will look overwhelmed by the width when you lay the doll on top of the pattern piece even if it is the right size, so before you trim make sure you have made allowances for the seams and the fact that buntings are bulky.
3. The length of the sleeves will also need adjusting. Measure the doll's arms from one wrist to the other wrist and cut sleeve piece according to that measurement.

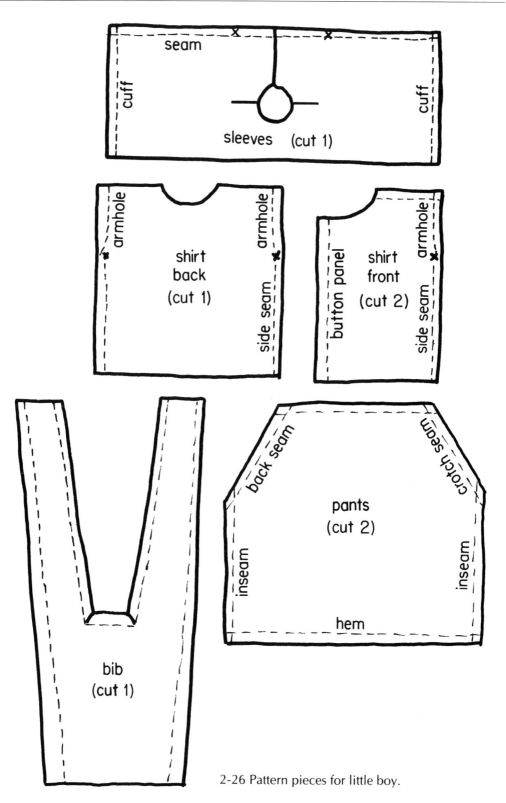

2-26 Pattern pieces for little boy.

2-27 Baby in bunting.

4. Only the shoulders need a good snug fit and the trimming can be done later. Cut down to size just before you do the final gluing.

Bunting Assembly

1. Make the sleeves as in all previous outfits, but make these directly on the doll's arms (omitting the step of gluing the sleeve on a pencil).

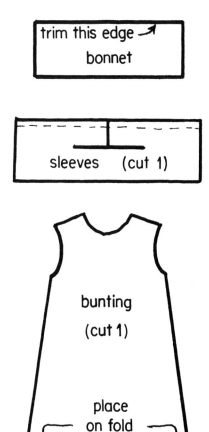

2-28 Bunting pattern pieces.

2. Glue bunting side seams and let dry thoroughly before turning right side out.
3. Slide the baby into the bunting. Trim the shoulder size if necessary before gluing the shoulder seams in place.

Baby Bonnet

1. Glue a strip of lace on inside of the hat piece so that the edge shows on the right side.
2. Place the strip of felt and lace on the doll's head with the lace side nearest the doll's head. Run the strip across the head from ear to ear, and glue it to the doll's head.
3. Glue down the back, folding the fabric like the end of a gift-wrapped box.

Now you have finished the whole process of making your own first family! You might see a couple of mistakes, but no one else will because they will be so charmed by your creations. The transformation is incredible. Your friends will not believe that these beautiful dolls had ever been in a dime store.

Section 11

DOLL BUILDING

Chapter 3   Heads and Faces

This chapter will describe two ways to make a doll's head. In the first method you will learn how to prepare and use a face mold. The second, and obviously more difficult, method will show you how to sculpt a head from a lump of clay.

Molded Faces

In the past, mold-making has been a chore that was time consuming, a little bit tricky and definitely quite messy. With new acrylic materials now on the market, it becomes much easier. The actual *making* of the mold takes about 30 seconds. This opens up a whole world of possibilities in doll-making. It makes many processes readily available to the beginner and gives the advanced dollmaker more opportunities for creative expression.

Although you will use an already-made face as the "original" for your mold, you will make your own doll's face from the mold. I can guarantee that no two people will make the same finished piece even if both start by using the same mold.

I would be quite surprised if *one* person made two identical finished dolls from the same mold.

The first step in this project will be to find a face that fills all the requirements of size and material. And, the most important requirement of all is: it has to be a face that you like! Then you will make a mold by taking an impression of this face with acrylic clay. After the mold has hardened, you will build the head and shoulders onto a wire armature.

Tools and Materials

Acrylic clay. The best type is brand-named Sculpey, and can be purchased in art supply stores.

Waxed paper.

Baby powder.

Paintbrush. An older medium-sized artist's brush is perfect.

Tool for smoothing clay. A nutpick works very well, but bobby pins, paper clips and small crochet hooks can be used.

Felt-tip marking pen.

Finding a Face

There are several things to consider when you look for a face to use for your doll mold. The scale must be one-inch-equals-one-foot, and the features must be in proportion. The face must be firm enough to hold its shape when the mold is being made. After these practical considerations have been taken into account, you can make some creative decisions. Who are you going to make, an old woman? a handsome young man? a child?

Although any size doll can be made with this technique, we are making dollhouse dolls and the scale is very important. Here, as in all phases of doll-making you can use yourself as a model by measuring your face and translating it to one-twelfth scale. If your face is 8 inches from hairline to chin, the doll's face would be about ⅔ inch, (8 inches is two-thirds of a foot). Most dollhouse dolls' faces measure between ⅝ inch and ¾ inch from hairline to chin but this measurement is very flexible, since real people come in so many different sizes. It is the face size, *not* the head size that is important. If you find a face you like and the features are in miniature scale and in proportion to the face you may use it, even though the full head is larger than scale. Look at other dollhouse dolls in stores, especially in room settings, and you will soon develop an eye for spotting pieces that are exactly in scale.

It is very important that the face you choose be made of a firm material, because the basic technique for making this type of mold is to press the acrylic clay onto the original to make the impression. Soft plastic or rubber would bend and distort the face in the process of mold-making. The face has to be made of porcelain or china, hard plastic, metal or another material that will hold its shape.

There are many places to look for little faces. Begin your search by looking at other dolls. The hard plastic dolls that you used to make gesso dolls in Section I often have potentially good facial shapes. However, the plastic material and the production line painting usually detract from the original form to such an extent that you can hardly tell that the structure of the face is quite good.

Many china figurines are in correct scale for dollhouse dolls. You may have some very valuable pieces decorating your home. They can safely be used for this type of mold-making. Inexpensive china figurines can be found in dime stores, discount stores or yard sales, and sometimes they have very interesting faces. Frequently a small face or figure is incorporated into the design of Victorian picture frames, lamps or furniture. Bronze and other cast metal figurines and lamps were quite popular in Victorian decor; some of these figures have lovely faces.

You can't always tell by looking at a figure what kind of a mold it will produce. Since the mold is so easy to make, the best thing to do is experiment. Make several molds from different faces and choose the one that excites your imagination.

Treasures of a
Toy Store delight
a small child.

A Toymaker
helps his
young customer.

A well-stocked General Store.

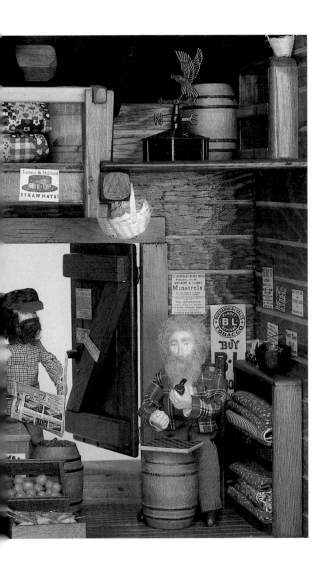

An old-time Post Office
in a corner of the
General Store.

Fashionable dolls exchange valentines. *Photograph by Alida Fish.*

A Baker
displays his
delectable goods.

A Street Peddler
with flowers
for sale.

Santa Playing the Cello by Jean Schram.
Courtesy of The Enchanted Doll House.

Owners of the
Fabric Store
serve their
customers.

Jazz Musicians play in a nightclub.

Hope's Harvest Shack by Hope Elliot. *Courtesy of The Enchanted Doll House.*

Your doll can have a beginning as humble as dime store china or as prestigious as the best piece in an antique collection. It really doesn't matter. What is important is the basic form of the face and how you handle it.

Making the Mold

There are a number of new materials that make it possible to skip many tiresome steps in mold-making. Acrylic clay (brand name Sculpey) is truly a miracle product. It feels like the traditional plasticine, or what I called "modeling clay" when I was a child. You can mold it, model it, stretch it, and shape it in almost any way until you bake it; then it becomes permanently hard. It can still be carved or sanded though. Another product introduced by the same company has the same qualities, but when it is baked it becomes rock hard (Super Sculpey). This material is especially good for making small parts of the body—such as fingers—unbreakable.

PREPARING THE CLAY. Start with a piece the size of a tennis ball (one bar of Sculpey). Roll it and pat it into a smooth solid ball. Press it down on a piece of waxed paper to flatten it to a disc that is one inch thick and two inches across. Carefully turn it over so that the smooth side next to the waxed paper is up. Make sure there are no cracks or lines in the surface. If there are, they can be smoothed over with your fingertips.

PREPARING THE ORIGINAL. To prepare the original face, dust it with baby powder or any other talcum. Using a large brush (#5), dip it into the powder and dust every bit of the surface of the face so it will not stick to the clay when you push it into the mold.

Draw an imaginary line from the middle of each ear, over the top of the head and down both sides of the neck and shoulders. This is the portion of the head that can be molded in a one-piece mold. If you make the mold any deeper or farther back on the head, you will make an "undercut," which will pull the rest of the face out of shape as it is being released

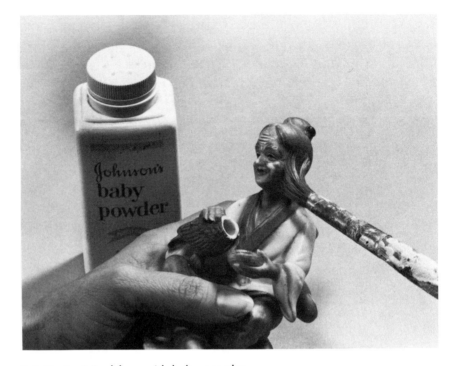

3-1 Dust original face with baby powder.

from the mold. Most of the faces on the figurines or dolls from which you will be making your molds were themselves cast in a mold. Their features have been made so that they will easily come out of the mold.

Sometimes you can use a carved wooden face to make the mold, but you do have to check to see that there are no undercuts in the face. If you can't tell by looking, give it a try. The worst that could happen is that you will have to roll up your clay and start over with a new face.

MAKING THE IMPRESSION. With your clay flat on the table, smooth side up, press your powdered original down into the clay disc until you reach the imaginary line (Fig. 3-2). Carefully pull the original *straight* up, without disturbing the clay. Now follow the manufacturer's directions for hardening the acrylic clay. The first time you bake acrylic clay it is a good idea to keep checking the oven every five minutes. Since each oven heats a little bit differently, yours might be too hot and the clay could cook too fast. If that happens, it will lose its smooth surface. After the mold is baked, let it cool for half an hour.

Mark the top, bottom and sides of the mold with a felt-tip pen (Fig. 3-3). This will be helpful later to help you center the face on the doll's head.

TESTING. You won't be able to tell if you have made a good mold until you take an impression from it. Dust the inside of the mold with baby powder just as you did with the figurine. There should only be a thin covering of powder in the mold. The powder tends to collect in the tip of the nose and in each crevice, so blow into the mold to remove excess powder. Be ready for a cloud of powder to come billowing out, but don't worry about blowing it all out; a thin layer will remain. Each time you use the mold, it must be dusted with powder which acts as a "mold release."

Break off a walnut-sized piece of clay; put it on the end of your thumb. Smooth the surface and push the clay into the mold (Fig. 3-4). You have to push hard! Then pull it straight out so the tiny features will not be bumped and distorted. The

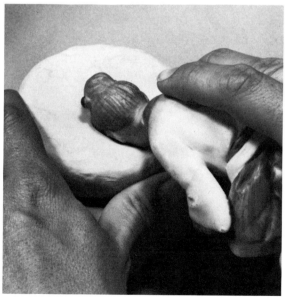

3-2 Press original firmly and evenly into clay.

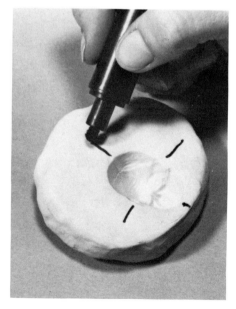

3-3 Mark the mold for easier centering.

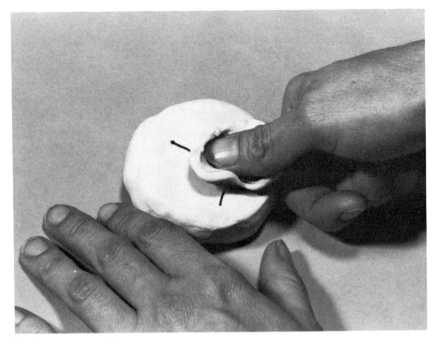

3-4 Testing the mold.

tip of the nose is the deepest point in the mold so if the nose doesn't come out it is probably because you didn't push the clay far enough into the mold. If you don't get a good impression, try again. Remember to dust the mold *each time* with powder. If there is a flaw in the face that comes up time after time, it's in the mold. If it's a small flaw, you can fix it by smoothing it over with your fingers. Otherwise you'll have to remake the mold.

The first time you pull a perfect little face out of a new mold you will experience such a feeling of satisfaction—I won't even try to tell you how much fun it is!

Making the Face

Before you mold the face, you must construct a wire armature that will serve as the doll's skeleton. Chapter 5 contains complete instructions on making the armature.

1. Make a solid cylinder of acrylic clay 2 inches long and 1 inch in diameter. Round the ends and roll the center

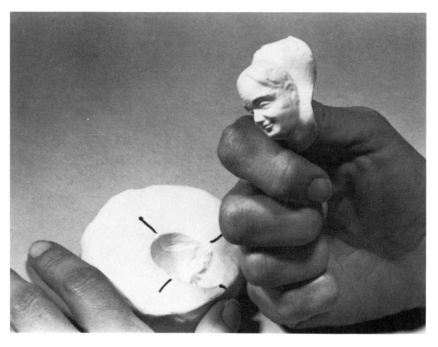

3-5 Check to be sure all features, especially the nose, have formed properly.

of the cylinder between your fingers to give it a slight hourglass shape. Make sure you keep the length of the cylinder about 2 inches.

2. One side of the top of the hourglass will form the face. Shape this side to a blunt point, and make the surface very smooth (Fig. 3-6). This blunt point will be pressed into the shape of the face in the mold. Having the point go in first helps the nose and chin to be completely formed.

3. Dust the inside of the mold with baby powder as you did when testing the mold. Dust your fingers as well to keep the clay from sticking to you.

4. Center the armature on the back of the hourglass with the wire intersection of the neck and shoulders over the narrow and lower part of the hourglass (Fig. 3-7).

5. Press the smooth, pointed side of the clay into the mold by placing your thumb over the back of the head

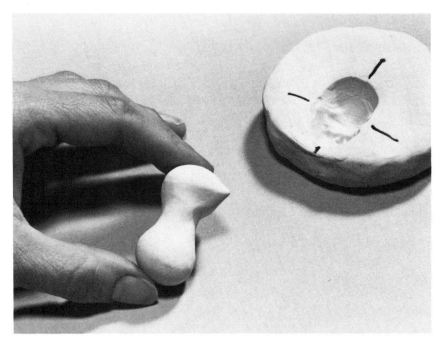

3-6 Form an hourglass with a blunt point on one end.

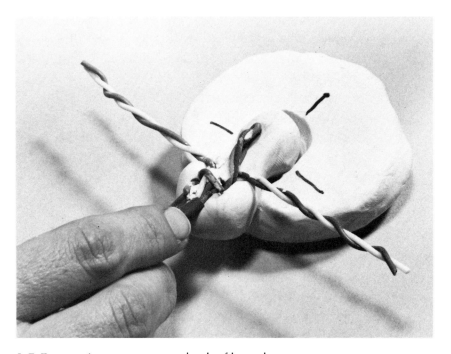

3-7 Center wire armature over back of hourglass.

and neck; *firmly* press wire and clay together into the mold (Fig. 3-8).

6. Remove your thumb without disturbing the clay. Carefully fold the excess clay which pushed out past the edges of your thumb toward the center of the head, covering the wires (Fig. 3-9 and 3-10).

7. Pull wire and clay straight up out of the mold (Fig. 3-11).

The placement of the head on the wire armature is a little tricky because it's not easy to guess the position of the face inside the mold after you have pressed in the clay. Unless your mold has good shoulder impressions, the placement of the head is a matter of trial and error. When you first look at the face you may find it is either too high or too low. It is easy to peel the soft clay off the armature, form it back into the hourglass shape and start over.

If you don't pull the armature and face straight out of the mold, the head will tip up so that the doll is looking at the sky

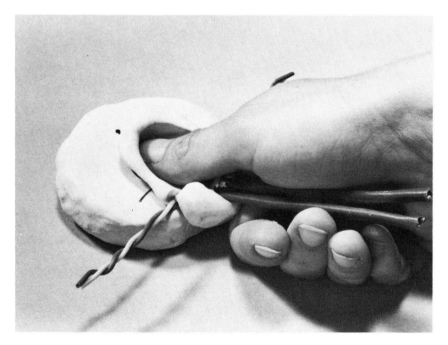

3-8 Press clay firmly into mold.

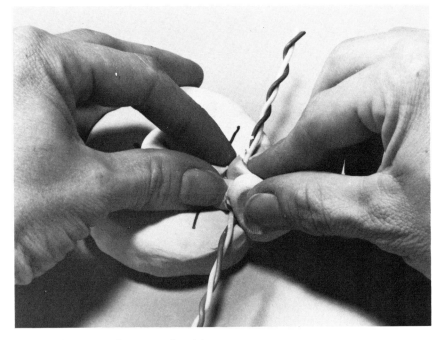

3-9 Pinch excess clay over shoulder armature.

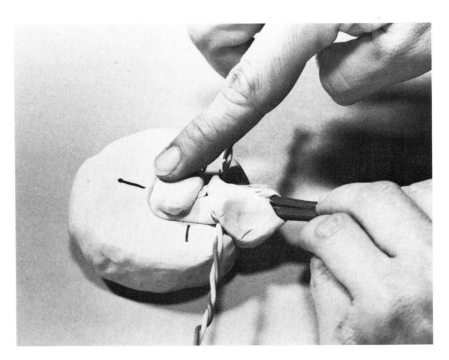

3-10 Fold excess clay down toward center of head.

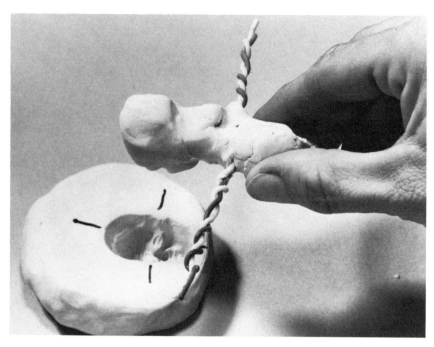

3-11 Pull clay straight up out of mold.

or down so she is looking at her feet. If this happens it usually can be corrected while the clay is still soft.

As you work with acrylic clay, the warmth of your hands makes the clay very soft. If you put it in the refrigerator for about 15 minutes, it will become much firmer and easier to work with.

FINISHING TOUCHES. Gently push, pat, and smooth the sides of the neck with the tips of your index fingers (Fig. 3-12). Push the excess clay toward the back and downward. A very gentle touch is required during this stage of modeling to avoid disturbing the parts already in place. Give the back of the head a rounded shape. Feel the back of your own head and neck. The neck goes up much farther in the back than in the front; the top of the back of the neck is almost even with the bottom of the nose (Fig. 3-13).

The hair is probably molded onto the head of the face you used to make the mold. In this project, you will put fiber hair on your doll, so you should gently push the grooves of the molded hair back into the head. Still using only the tips of

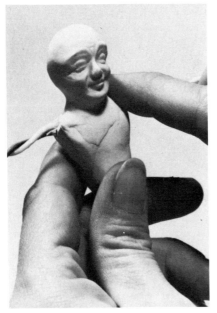

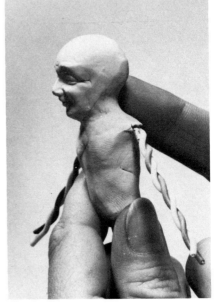

3-12 Gently smooth the neck.   3-13 Round the back of the head.

your fingers, softly smooth the surface of the head with short strokes. Do not apply pressure; use the same stroke you would use if you were petting a tiny kitten. Use this same stroke again all around the edge of the molded face; smoothing the clay toward the back of the head.

Pack clay around the wire intersections which form the shoulders and chest area to secure the connections. You don't have to model shoulders and chest, because these parts will be made with polyester filling later. Right now all you have to do is secure the wires with the clay and make the clay even on both sides, front and back so you will have an even foundation to build the shoulders and chest on when the time comes.

There are usually impressions in the mold for eyes. They may be as simple as small circles or they can be very complicated with eyelashes and wrinkled eyelids. You have to take a good long look at those eyes to decide if you can use them as they are on your doll. This depends on how clearly the definition of the eye has carried over from the original to the mold and finally to your doll. If the shape has held up throughout the molding process and the eyes are clear, your head and face are complete.

If the eyes have been distorted and seem smudged or unclear, use a nutpick, the end of a paper clip, or any other small tool to smooth over the eyes (Fig. 3-14). Make a very smooth surface so when the time comes to paint the eyes you won't be painting on bumps. Be careful not to disturb the eyebrow line, the cheek bones, or the bridge of the nose.

When you are all finished, bake the doll in the oven just as you did the mold. Follow directions on the package but check occasionally to make sure it isn't baking too fast. Allow the head to cool at least half an hour before continuing work on your doll.

Sculptured Heads

A more difficult, and to some more rewarding, method of head-building is sculpture. You become totally responsible for the final appearance of the face. Some dollmakers will enjoy

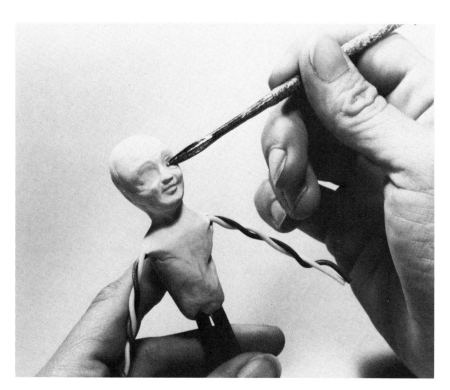

3-14 Smooth over eyes if necessary.

this challenge, while others will be happy trying the endless variations of mold-making.

Before you dismiss sculpture as being too difficult, you should at least try it—including hardening the clay and painting on a face. It is not necessary to be a Michelangelo to create expressive, beautiful dollhouse dolls. Because of the small scale, faces do not have to be as detailed as in the larger sculpture that most people are familiar with. And the painting can often transform a simple face into a seemingly detailed rendition.

Carefully follow the steps outlined in this section, and I am sure you will be pleased with the results. And you can only get better with practice.

Materials

There is a great variety of materials used for dollmaking. The following four are the kinds that can be comfortably used at home: acrylic clay (Sculpey), self-hardening clay, papier-mâché and homemade composition.

ACRYLIC CLAY AND SELF-HARDENING CLAY. These are very similar in handling and effect. Both types of clay have the advantage of producing a very smooth surface, which is essential for a doll's face that requires fine detail in the features. The main difference between the two clays is in the curing. Acrylic clay is heat-treated or baked to harden it. It will not dry when exposed to air. Self-hardening clay will harden *only* when exposed to air.

Use only acrylic-based paints with acrylic clay; oil paints or latex paints will not dry properly. Both types of clay are ready to use straight from the package.

PAPIER-MÂCHÉ. There are papier-mâché dolls and puppets in antique collections that are hundreds of years old. It is a well respected medium. Some of these doll's faces have very fine features and smooth surfaces. But getting a smooth surface with papier-mâché means a lot of work. You will have to apply several layers of gesso between numerous sandings. If you are just beginning to work with papier-mâché, I suggest that you take advantage of the rough texture that is a characteristic of the medium. Character dolls often have faces that will work well in papier-mâché.

Papier-mâché can be bought ready to mix with water, or made from scratch with the following recipe.

Ingredients:

    2 to 4 rolls of white toilet tissue

    1 cup prepared wallpaper paste

Directions:

    Feed tissue into paste, one ply at a time. Stir continuously, then knead until mixture reaches consistency for modeling.

COMPOSITION. Another mâché that has a long history in doll-making is composition. Composition is a catch-all phrase that decribes a modeling or molding substance which is made of many particles of wood or straw held together with any kind of glue that dries to a very hard finish. Long ago doll artists used any material available to make composition. They used wood chips or straw and sometimes stuck it all together with molasses!

You can make your own composition, too, by mixing sawdust with white glue according to the recipe given here. It can be as fine as the sawdust you use. It is easy to mix and fairly easy to handle, but not as smooth or easy as clay. When it is dry, the doll's head is practically indestructible.

Ingredients:

    1 handful of sawdust (finest texture possible)

    White woodworkers' glue

Directions:

    Dampen sawdust thoroughly with water. Squeeze excess water out of the sawdust. Add white glue and mix. Keep adding glue until mixture holds together well enough for modeling.

Shaping the Head

Begin this doll with the wire armature described in Chapter 5. Build an hourglass shape out of clay, similar to the one in Fig. 3-6 (without the point), directly onto the wire armature.

Shape the head into an egg shape (Fig. 3-15). Be careful not to stretch the neck and make it too long. You might find that it is easier to model the head first and then put it on the wire. Just make sure the connection between head and body, otherwise known as the neck, is secure and firm and the surface is free of cracks, bumps and folds.

Mark the face for the placement of the features. Using a pinpoint as a drawing tool, make a faint, vertical line down the center of the face, which divides it into two equal halves. Then divide the face into thirds with horizontal score marks (fig. 3-16). Divide the top and bottom thirds into halves with horizontal lines. These lines will tell you exactly where to place the features (fig. 3-17).

Modeling the Features

During the whole process of modeling the head and the face, keep turning the head and the face from side to side. Look at it upside-down occasionally to help you keep the face from becoming lopsided, which can easily happen if you look at your doll and work on it from one point of view. Always

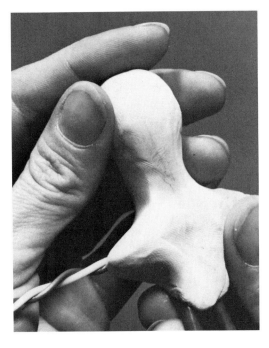

3-15 Shaping the head.

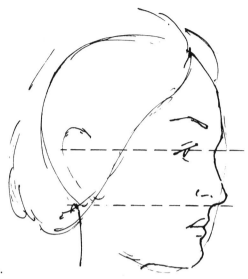

3-16 Divide the face into thirds.

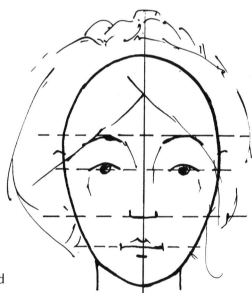

3-17 Divide the top and bottom thirds into halves.

take the time to stop, hold the doll at arm's length and analyze your work.

EYES. Using a nutpick or a metal crochet hook, push the clay in to make indentations for eyes (fig. 3-18). Make these smooth indentations on either side of the center vertical line and directly below the eyebrow line.

Nose. As you push in to make the places for the eyes, a nose will emerge between the two indentations. Pull this clay out slightly and down to form the nose (fig. 3-19). You may find that you have to add a tiny ball of clay (or whatever material you're using) to the end of the nose. Use a *very* small piece; a piece the size of a pinhead can make a big difference. You will need a pointed tool to push in the areas at either side of the nose. This defines the nose and begins the shape of the cheeks. Check the mirror and feel the contours of your face with your fingertips.

Cheeks. The cheeks come out, a raised, rounded surface. Here again, you may need to add some clay. Add an equal amount to each side of the face before you start smoothing and blending the surface. The character you are creating determines the shape of the cheeks and where you add extra

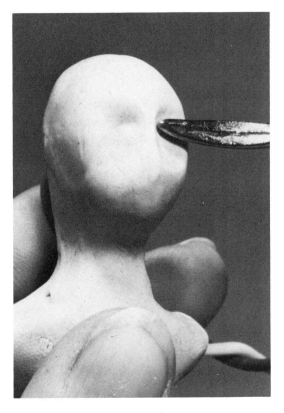

3-18 Making indentations for eyes.

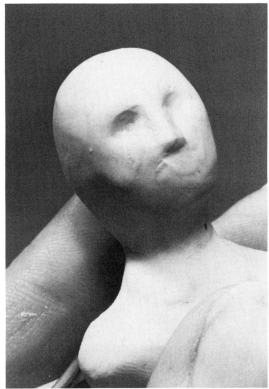

3-19 Forming the nose.

clay. For very high cheekbones—an American Indian or a fashion model—add the clay just beneath the corners of the eyes and blend it out to the sides. If you are making a chubby child or a jazz trumpet player, the full cheeks begin directly under the eyes and are full all the way down to the mouth and beyond the jawline.

JAWLINE. To make the chin take a look at your own jaw. The jawbone is the only bone or shape that is separate from the shape of the skull. The jawbone juts out from the egg shape of the skull. You might already have enough clay on the head to push it around and up to form a good chin. Or you might have to add a piece. One of the main structural differences between the faces of men and women is that men have more prominent jawlines. They are lower and more square.

MOUTH. To form the mouth take a look at the line you drew across the center of the lower third of the face. This is the line where the lips meet. You have to examine the face and make a decision. Is there enough clay under the nose to give the mouth shape? If your doll looks like he has taken his false

3-20 Two different types of cheeks.

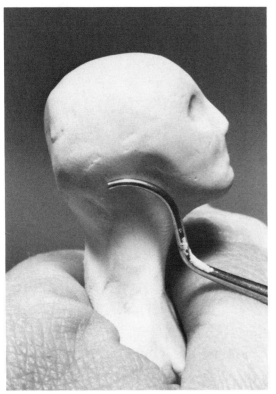

3-21 Forming chin and jawline.

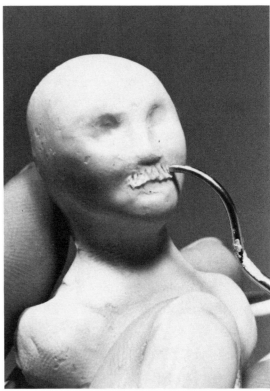

3-22 Adding moustache for male doll.

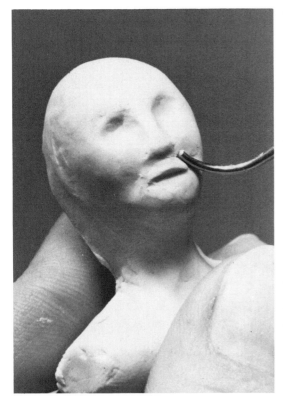

3-23 Adding clay to form upper lip.

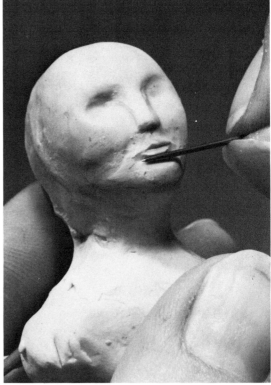

3-24 Forming lower lip with pin.

teeth out and the space between the chin and the nose is quite sunken, you will need to add a small piece of clay. An easy solution to the problem for a man doll is to add a moustache (fig. 3-22).

If you are making a woman, child or a clean-shaven man, shape a tiny semicircle of clay and add it directly under the nose (fig. 3-23). This forms the upper jaw and top lip. Blend the edges of the semicircle to the edge of the cheek, keeping that plane as a separate shape. Don't lose the planes of the cheeks by filling in with clay and making the area straight across. Use a straight pin or dental tool for this delicate work. Using the side of your tool, make the dent between the bottom lip and chin (feel that space on your own chin) and gently roll the tiny bit of clay upward to form the bottom lip (fig. 3-24). Use your tool to even up the corners of the mouth or bring both corners up to make a smile.

Create a dimple in the chin by pushing in a little dent in the center with a pinhead and very gently pinching the dent

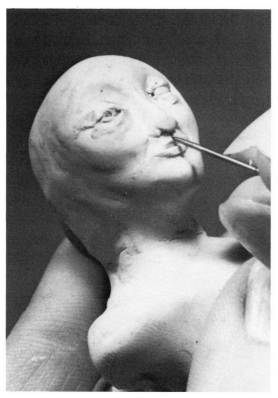

3-25 Forming ridges above mouth.

3-26 Modeling the eyes.

together. Make nostrils by sticking a pinpoint up each one and then gently push back down to reshape the nose. Above your top lip (feel it) there are two little vertical ridges. If you use a pinhead to make a round dent directly below the center of the nose and centered above the mouth, you will create that shape (fig. 3-25).

MODELING THE EYES. Work on both eyes at the same time; do each step on one eye, then the other eye. This will help to make eyes that match.

Start with two tiny balls, eyeballs to be exact. Place them in their rightful places on either side of the nose and centered under the eyebrow line. Lightly push them onto the surface of the face, just enough so they will stick.

Roll two more balls about the same size as the eyeballs. Flatten them on your waxed paper and cut them in half. These half circles will be the upper and lower eyelids.

Press the eyelids in place on the eyeballs with the corners meeting at the tearducts and the outside corners of the eyes (fig. 3-26). Even up the spaces where the eyeballs show through so both eyes are the same size.

Smooth the outside edges of the eyelids so they blend with the surface of the face.

Use a pinpoint to draw a line (make a score mark) along the upper eyelid to give it stronger definition and make an eyelash line. Make a pinpoint in each eyeball to represent the pupil. Make sure both eyes are looking in the same direction.

The eyes are a difficult part of the face to model in miniature. If the process seems too frustrating, you can smooth the clay over and leave a good surface for painting the eyes in place. Painted eyes are very effective and they will match the rest of the face. Don't be discouraged if you have decided to skip this modeling step. Later in your doll-making career you can use these instructions on a larger doll.

Chapter 4 **Face Painting and Hair**

You are now going to put the finishing touches on your doll's head. The more-detailed clay heads rely less on painted features than did the dime-store doll in Section I. But the subtle changes you can add with paint will often make dramatic differences in your doll's character.

"Real" fiber hair will be your doll's crowning glory. Modern materials can be used to fashion almost any hairstyle you can imagine.

If you are modeling hands and feet out of clay that must be baked to harden, do these before completing the head. Some of the materials might not hold up to the heat.

You paint your doll the same way as was described in Chapter 1. The big difference now is taking each step a little bit further, exploring the significant changes that subtle shades of color can make. You will also learn how to change the facial expression and character of your doll through painting.

Painting

Little changes cause great differences when working at this scale. The slant of the eyes can change the expression of the whole face. When you paint with acrylics and are not pleased with the results, you can easily cover your work with another layer of paint; so feel free to take risks—give each idea a try!

Choosing Colors

Before you start painting think about the character of your doll and exactly which colors you want to use. Look closely at people you know, people on TV and in books and magazines. Various ethnic groups have different skin tones; these are obvious differences. But if you explore the *subtle* gradations in people, you will be able to portray these little "characters" in a much more effective way.

After you have been looking at people for a while, you will begin to see that most people have different skin color-ings. Outdoor types—sportsmen, farmers, old seafaring men (and friends who have moved to Florida), have tanned or weathered skin colors. People with dark eyes and hair, or Mediterranean ancestry have "olive" colored skin. The Irish are sometimes characterized by pale skin and very rosy cheeks. Older people are often pale. A sheltered young lady used to be excessively pale, because ladies and gentlemen did not have to work in the hot sun. Nowadays, the reverse is true. A modern lady of leisure has a deep tan—a sign that she does not have to go to work at a job indoors.

As you are looking at people and noticing the subtle color differences, you will also notice that natural colors are often quite dull. When the colors were being handed out, human beings did not have the same good fortune as red cardinals, goldfish, green frogs or bluejays. The colors of people are not the pure and beautiful colors flowing from tubes of paint. Even the bluest of eyes do not achieve the pure color of Cobalt Blue or Ultramarine. In dollmaking, we can idealize colors to a certain extent, but if we take it too far, the illusion is lost. You can use more blue than is naturally found in blue eyes, but if you use pure blue straight out of the tube, it will look garish.

For natural-looking colors that blend in with the entire face, you will have to tone down *every* color. Tone down means mixing in a little bit of raw umber or black. There is only one exception: if you are making a woman doll, you can give her bright red lips and rosy cheeks because some women wear brightly colored make-up.

Aside from make-up colors, remember to tone down all the colors to make them blend together. Each color you use on the face must be carefully chosen and mixed to harmoniously relate to all the other colors.

Mixing Fleshtones

Use the same basic formula for mixing fleshtone as you did for your first doll: 90 percent white, 5 percent cadmium red, and 5 percent yellow ochre. Most skin colors are variations on this formula. Start with a very small amount of white. Add much smaller quantities of cadmium red and yellow ochre in equal amounts until the color looks like fleshtone. It can be varied as follows:

> Suntanned or weathered skin—add a little burnt sienna.
> Pale complexion—add more white and use more red than ochre so that the skin doesn't have a yellowish tinge.
> Ruddy skin—use more red than ochre.
> Olive skin—use slightly more ochre than red and add burnt sienna.
> Oriental skin—use more yellow ochre and a little bit of burnt sienna.
> Negro skin colors—use *only* Burnt Sienna and Raw Umber mixed with clear gel medium. To lighten the color use more clear gel. Don't use white: it will make a chalky unnatural skin tone.

After you have chosen the skin tone for your doll, some experimenting will have to be done. Mix the colors and let them dry to show exactly how they will look on the doll. The colors will darken slightly as they dry.

You will have to experiment with the consistency of the paint too. The paint should be thin enough so the brush does not leave any marks, which would be serious distortions on such a little face. A drop of water will do the job of thinning if the paint is too thick. If the paint is too thin it will be runny, uncontrollable and transparent.

After you have thought about the fleshtone, mixed it and experimented with it on scrap paper, paint the head, shoulders, hands and face of your doll. Take special care to put a very thin layer on the features. Use two coats of paint if the color of the clay shows through. Wait a few minutes between coats to make sure the first coat is thoroughly dry, because if you start the second coat *too soon* the partially dry paint will become rough and bumpy. Save the leftover fleshtone in a plastic bag. It will not dry out for several days and you might need it for touch-ups.

Sketching the Features

The face is completed structurally. Now you emphasize the features with color. Unless you are very confident in your brush technique, begin painting the features by sketching them in pale yellow.

EYES. Follow the molded surface for the eyelash and eyebrow lines unless you have chosen to make a smooth surface for the eyes. In this case you will have to create the eyes totally with paint. Look at the face you used to make the mold to help you with the placement.

LIPS. Fill in the lips by following the mold. Then if you want to, you can change the shape of the mouth (and the expression of the whole face), by turning up the corners of the mouth for more of a smile. Make the lips fuller or thinner to reinforce the unique mood of your character.

When the features are all in place you are ready to start adding the little bit of color that makes the big difference.

Painting the Eyes

The eyes are probably the most difficult to paint so have your clean, damp sponge handy. In between steps, let the paint dry thoroughly, so if you do need to make a correction with the sponge you will remove only the wet paint; the paint which has dried will stay in place. (Refer to fig. 1-13.)

1. Start by painting a white almond-shaped eyeball under each eyelash line. The next two lines—the eyelash and the eyebrow—are extremely important to the expression of the whole face.
2. Paint the eyelash line with burnt umber.
3. Paint the eyebrows the same color as the hair will be. Use a very fine line for a woman. A series of overlapping dots makes a bushy, masculine eyebrow. (See fig. 1-14.)
4. To paint the tiny circle representing the iris of your doll's eye follow these steps (practice on a piece of scrap paper, which you have *painted white*):
   a. Choose the color and tone it down with raw umber. Burnt sienna can be used all alone for brown eyes.
   b. Mix the paint so it is a little bit more watery than the paint you used for the fleshtone.
   c. Fill the brush with paint and very lightly touch the tip of the bristle to the center of the almond-shaped eyeball.
   d. The watery paint will run off the brush and form a perfect circle. The size of the circle (iris) depends on how long you let the brush touch the surface. In your practice you will develop the feel of handling the watery paint.
   e. When you do the second eye be very careful to place the circle in the same spot; it is difficult to make the eyes look in the same direction.

Painting the Mouth

For a purely natural look, the lip color can be mixed from cadmium red, white, and burnt sienna. This can be used on

men or women with natural coloring. For women use less burnt sienna in the mixture. Adding burnt sienna makes pink richer and more natural looking. For lipstick colors, cadmium red medium is *the* red! Add a touch of white and any shade of pink that you desire is yours. Add a tiny bit of orange for coral colors. If you are using lipstick colors don't forget to consider the color of the dress your little lady will be wearing. Make sure there will be no clashes between clothes and make-up!

With the color you have chosen and mixed, paint the lip color over the yellow sketching. When you are satisfied with the shape of the lips, mix a little bit of burnt umber with the lip color to darken the color just a shade. Paint a thin line of darker color along the line where the lips meet. This will make the lips look more "real."

Some professional dollmakers believe a doll is not really finished unless the nostrils and tear ducts are painted. The colors you will use are the same as those you used for natural lips—white, red and burnt sienna. Paint small elongated dots for nostrils and very, very tiny dots for tear ducts.

Character Dolls

When you are doing "character" dolls you can add quite a bit to the personality with just a few extra touches of color. You can make wrinkles and freckles, moustaches and make-up by painting them.

Wrinkles are very subtle lines. The color is white with very small amounts of black and raw umber. Make the value, which is the amount of black or white in the mixture, just a little darker than that of the skin. If you make the wrinkle lines too dark they will stand out and look like a net on the face. Paint a couple of wavy lines on the forehead, "crows feet" by the eyes, and a line on either side of the mouth.

You can put together a mixture of white, black and blue to make darker areas under the eyes. Use this as a "wash," which is a very watery mixture of paint. The paint underneath is supposed to show through. Use a tissue to blot excess paint.

If you want to change the character of your beautiful lady to that of a "floozie" or "painted lady," exaggerate the lip size slightly and use a very bright color. Paint tiny black eyelashes on the eyeline. Add a black beauty mark below the corner of the eye or above the corner of the mouth.

If you want to create a totally different type of character, paint on freckles and a peaches-and-cream complexion and make her into the farmer's daughter.

If you are making character dolls, you must do more "people watching." Notice and remember the little details that typify a character and add them to your doll. You can do some of them in painting. Later, you can add further details through accessories, glasses, cigars, jewelry or hats.

So much can be done to create a character through painting the face. Look at what the Old Masters did on a flat piece of canvas! As *you* master painting skills, you can go into more and more detail when you paint your doll's face.

Hair

Usually the most desirable miniature pieces are the most realistic looking. "Real" hair is a big plus in making dolls look more like real people.

This section explains how to find good doll hair and how to use it. There are very simple hairstyles and some pretty complicated ones too. I hope you have a good time as you take your doll into your miniature beauty salon and give her "real" hair.

Tools and Materials

Fabric glue.
Scissors.
Round toothpicks.
Straight pins.
Waxed paper.
Acrylic spray.

Among your craft supplies you will probably find polyester fiber used for pillow stuffing. It can be used for white hair only because, like other synthetics, it refuses to absorb dye.

Cotton batting from your medicine chest is just the opposite. The porous cotton fibers absorb color quickly. If you want honey blond, dip it in a cup of tea. Mix a little bit of black ink with water for gray dye. The trouble with cotton batting is that it is made from extremely fine, short fibers. Hairstyles are limited to simple ones because the mass of fibers will not hold together.

Another excellent possibility for hair for your doll is an old wig or hairpiece that has long since lost its place as a fashion accessory. These pieces can be very useful if the hair isn't too coarse; you can tell by draping a lock of hair over the doll's head.

The best place to look for doll hair is your yarn box. Find a good color—not too bright, and in character for your doll. Natural fibers, cotton or wool, behave better when you are working them into hairdos; but synthetics are sometimes quite good, too. Once again, you must experiment.

To make yarn into a material you can use for doll hair, you must undo the work of the spinner, and return it to its original state: many long fibers, lined up side by side.

1. Cut several strands of yarn 12 inches long.
2. Submerge them in a dishpan of warm water and untwist or "unspin" each strand underwater.
3. Try to keep the strings of wavy yarn lined up side by side, and let them soak for approximately half an hour.
4. Try to blend the strands by rubbing the fibers together between your fingers.
5. Stack the pile of wavy strings of hair together and let dry overnight.
6. After they are dry, blend them together more.
7. If you want the wavy hair to stay wavy, skip Steps 8 and 9.
8. Take a good grip on each end of the whole pile and give it a series of short jerky yanks until it comes apart in the middle.
9. Pull it apart and lay one pile of fiber on top of the other. Straighten and smooth the fibers and then pull

them apart in the same way you did the first time.

10. The fibers should be separated from each other but still all going in the same direction.
11. To keep the hair flat and straightened, iron it between two sheets of waxed paper.

Hair that is made for dolls is sometimes very good and sometimes way under par. Be careful of colors that are too brash or hair that is too shiny. You really have to see it to tell if it is the right color and texture for natural-looking doll hair.

If you have a costume shop in your town, you are in luck!! Costume shops sell many natural shades of "fake" hair for dressing up real people, so the quality of the hair must be realistic. Large variety stores or Joke shops sometimes carry these same supplies. Contact the local theater group and find out where they order hair.

There is one time of year when all dime stores, discount or department stores are full of inexpensive items which radically change one's appearance—Halloween. This is a good time to stock up on doll hair. Examine all the masks, false beards and moustaches for good colors.

Any hairstyle must start with a good foundation. The two following "starts" will provide the necessary basic beginning for creating any hairstyle for your doll.

Part Lines

Start with a piece of doll hair that is 8 inches long, 2 inches wide and thick enough so when you are holding it tightly between your fingers it is 1/16 inch thick. Flatten and smooth this pile of fibers which we will refer to as a hank of hair. Always try to keep it as neat as possible.

To make a center part, sew a seam with the same color thread right across the center of the hair—on the sewing machine (Fig. 4-1). Divide the hair in half lengthwise along each side of the seam (Fig. 4-2). Then press the opposite halves together to hide the stitches; the seam becomes a very real-looking part.

4-1 Sew a seam across hair.
4-2 Divide hair in half lengthwise
and press opposite sides together.

As you are working on the hair, there will come moments when it is necessary to lay the doll down on the table and do something else. You can't lay it down on the back of the head anymore because you will have wet glue there. Or you will have curls or a French twist that you do *not* want to become flat. The solution is to push the doll's arms straight in front and let it rest on its toes and hands as if it were doing "push-ups."

This position keeps the whole head and body suspended and very securely situated until the wet area dries. These "push-ups" will also come in handy when dressing the doll.

Put the hair aside for a moment because it takes both hands to put on the glue. Look at yourself in the mirror to observe your hairline. You will have to make the hair cover the ears on your doll whether you are doing a woman's or a man's hairstyle because your doll probably doesn't have ears. Use a stiff brush and paint glue all along the doll's hairline. Fill in the entire surface of the head with glue. Always stick the hair to the glue gently so the glue doesn't come through to the outside layer of hair.

Attaching the Hair

1. Center the stitches (part) on the top of the doll's head.
2. Stick the edges along the glued hairline in front.
3. Work the edges of the hair together in the back so they blend.

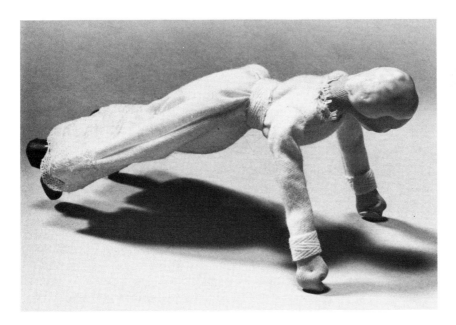

4-3 Put doll in "push-up" position when working on head.

4-4 Attaching hair to head.

4. Smooth the sides and back down so the hair adheres to the doll's head all the way down to the hairline in back.
5. Move the hair around with a straight pin to make sure it is even.

Simple Twist Hairline

Take a piece of "hair" the same size used for the sewing machine start—8 inches by 2 inches by 1/16 inch. Flatten it and smooth it. It is very important to keep fibers from getting "messy" because they become more difficult to straighten out as the hairdo evolves. It is impossible to keep the hair perfectly neat because it is unruly by nature—just do your best!

Set the hair aside for a moment and apply the glue to the doll's head, as in the previous section. Put your doll in the push-up position. Don't forget to wipe the glue off your fingers.

1. Take the piece of hair you have prepared. Hold it tightly in the center on the top between your thumbs and index fingers—thumbs side by side and on top.
2. Leave your left hand in the above position and still

holding tightly to the hair, twist your right hand around away from you so that your right index finger ends up on top, and your right thumb is on the bottom (Fig. 4-5). Then slide your left thumb over the "twist" to hold it in position (Fig. 4-6).

3. Center the middle of the twist on top of the head.
4. Pull the hair down in the front and stick it to the glue which forms the hairline.

This is almost the same as in the first method. The big difference is that you have to make sure the twist doesn't come undone before the whole head of hair has been fixed in place with glue. Even up the hair with a straight pin.

POMPADOUR. If you want a pompadour effect, take a few steps back to the beginning of the twisted hairline. Instead of twisting the hair once, twist it twice to form a tiny roll. Keep it tight. That tiny roll is centered on the hairline in front (Fig. 4-7). The rest of the hair is worked along the hairline and back. Press gently to the glued head so the glue doesn't come through.

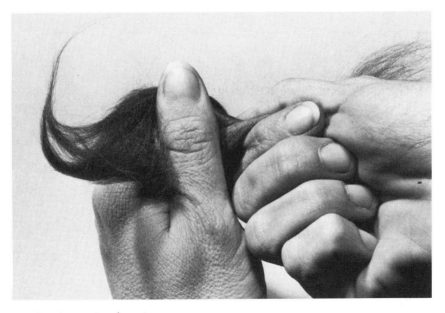

4-5 Starting a simple twist.

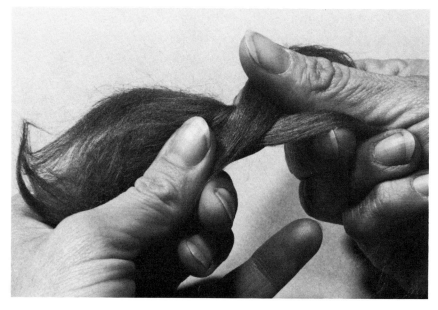

4-6 Simple twist ready to go on doll.

There are a variety of hairstyles to choose from, and several are discussed below. Before you proceed, there is one paramount rule: once the doll's hair is in place, let it dry thoroughly before you try to do the remainder of the hair-

4-7 Pompadour hairstyle.

styling. Actually, when the beginning of the hairdo is in place, that can be the end in itself. Long hair hanging straight down is perfect for a little girl or a modern young woman.

Braids

Braids that hang down on either side of the head, also known as pigtails, are made by dividing the hair in half and braiding each side. The only difference here is that you should try to keep the braid in the same position it will be in when the hairstyle is finished. If you braid the hair out away from the head as you do when braiding a real child's hair, it might have a tendency to stick out.

If you plan a hairstyle with the braids on top of the head, then that *would* be the way to do it. When they are done they will look like they belong there. Glue them in place, tuck the ends under, and snip off the excess if necessary. Fig. 4-13 show braids wrapped around the head.

One large single braid down the back is a very easy hairstyle. Women in Victorian days wore their hair in loose braids for sleeping. If you pull the single braid straight up the back, tuck the end in toward the head and glue in place, the braid becomes much fancier. Use pins to hold while drying.

For even more elaborate braided hairstyles, you can make a separate braid and attach it to the hair-do. Sometimes you can add a braid to camouflage an accidental bald spot or messy area. If you end up with a better looking hairstyle after covering mistakes, more power to you.

French Twist

The French twist is a popular and easy hairstyle. Draw the hair to the nape of the neck, and twist it around and around until it is snug (Fig. 4-8). Pull the twisted portion of the hair straight up and around until it is up the back of the head. If it feels too loose when you pull it up, give it one more twist (Fig. 4-9). Tuck the top under the rest of the twisted hair at the crown. Glue the twist in place and secure with straight pins while drying. It's much easier to move the hair into place with a straight pin than with your fingers. The hair doesn't stick to

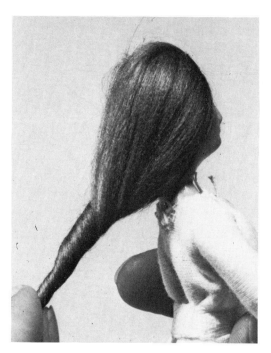

4-8 Twist hair until it is tight.

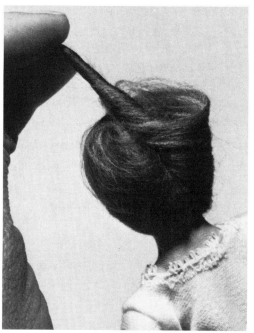

4-9 Pull twist straight up the back of head.

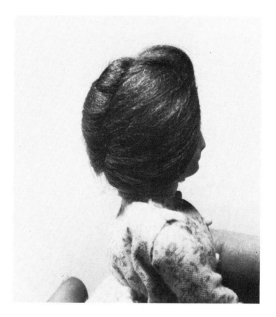

4-10 A finished French twist.

the pins like it does to your fingers and when you get the hair in position, the pin is right there ready to hold it until the glue dries.

Chignon

A chignon is created by gathering the hair together in one long piece, twisting it or rolling it around itself, thus forming it into a bun or knot on the back of the head. It can be large or small. It can sit right on top of the head or at the nape of the neck or anywhere in between. Some hairstyles can have more than one bun. Some are a combination of buns, twists, braids, and curls. You often see buns circled with braids, especially in Spanish hairstyles. The following instructions are for making a bun; you can decide on the size and position.

1. Choose the place on the head you want the bun to be.
2. Gather the hair and start twisting it from that point in much the same way you twisted the hair at the nape of the neck to begin the French twist.
3. When the hair is twisted tightly, stick a pin into the head in the center of the spot you have chosen for the bun.
4. Wrap the twisted hair around the pin until the bun reaches the size you desire.
5. Tuck the end under and trim if necessary.
6. Secure with glue and hold it with straight pins all around the bun.

Curls

One of the best things about curls is that they look so cute in miniature. They can dress up an ordinary hairstyle; they can hide little mistakes; and anyone who sees your curly haired doll will say, "Oh! How did you make those little tiny curls?"

Use the same material you have been using for hair. Snythetic materials are unpredictable as to whether or not the curling process will work. Natural fibers always work. Experimentation is the only way to find out.

Use round wooden toothpicks for "curlers." For each toothpick, use a tiny amount of hair—only a few strands—4 inches long. If you use too much, the hair will spring back and unwind itself. The amount of hair is something you will have to try until you get the hang of it.

1. Hold the end of the piece of hair and the end of the toothpick between the thumb and index finger of your left hand.
2. Turn the other end of the toothpick with your right hand.
3. After you have turned the toothpick around twice begin slowly sliding the thumb and index finger of your left hand toward the other end of the toothpick. Keep the hair tightly and evenly clamped to the toothpick as it circles around (Fig. 4-11).
4. When you come to the end of the hair, or the end of the toothpick, spin it a couple of times so the fibers of hair will stick to each other and hold the whole "curl" in place. Do several of these curls.
5. Dunk them in warm water, blot them dry and let them

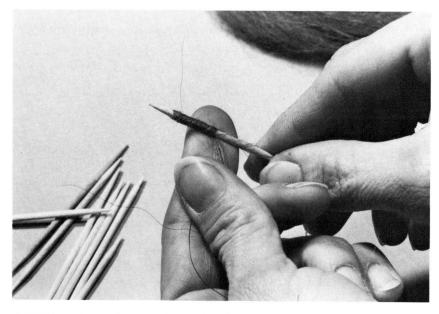

4-11 Wrapping curls around a toothpick.

dry overnight. You can put them in the sun or any warm cozy place in your house to speed up drying time. But don't put them in the oven! Some fibers, synthetic or natural, have a very low melting point.

6. Slip the toothpick out of the roll of hair.

7. Cut across the roll of hair, slicing it into 1/16-inch pieces. Each piece is a separate ringlet (Fig. 4-12).

8. The curls are incorporated into the hairstyle by putting a tiny dot of glue on the head or directly on the hair. Pick up a curl with a pair of tweezers and put it in place.

You can make an entire hairdo out of curls. Start with a bald doll and use the same gluing method you used for starting the other hairstyles. Put glue all over the doll's head, taking special care to make the hairline even. If you make the glue

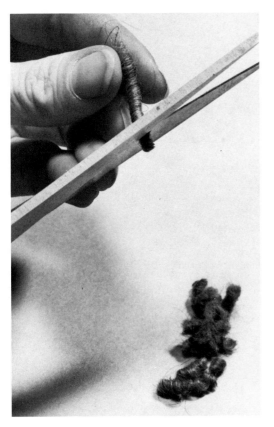

4-12 Cutting tiny curls.

hairline closer to the face, it will give the doll a more youthful look.

Cover the entire glued surface with curls. You will need about eight toothpicks full of curls for this hairstyle. If you want to make the curls a little larger, cut the curls in ⅛-inch pieces.

All of the hairstyles need to be "set" when you are all finished with them, but don't use hairspray. The alcohol in the hairspray will dissolve the paint on the face. Use clear acrylic spray coating. Several thin layers are always better than one thick one.

For authentic period styles, check the costume history books. You can duplicate the hairstyles of any of the historical

beauties by analyzing the components of the hairdo and following the steps for making each part.

Men and Boys

These male hairstyles are very simple because, traditionally, the emphasis is not on the hair in fashions for men.

The most simple and characterful man's hair treatment is the old gent with a rather large bald spot. White or gray hair is good to use for this one, but any color is appropriate.

Hair Around the Bald Spot

1. Measure from ear to ear, around the back of the head. Then add ½ inch.

4-13 A variety of hairstyles.

2. Use a piece of hair that length and ½ inch wide.
3. Put a strip of glue around the back of the head, starting in front of the place where an ear would be and continue around the back of the head to the front of the other ear.
4. Put the doll in the "push-up" position.
5. Fold the ends of the strip of doll hair under ¼ inch on each end.
6. Place the hair over the glued spot and gently push it into place.

Use small "snips" of hair for a moustache. Curled hair makes a good beard. On a young man doll with dark hair, a moustache and a beard offsets the bald spot, to give the whole effect a more balanced look.

The "whole head of curls" hairdo for women can also be done on your man. This hairdo is very cute on a little boy, too. With large full curls, he can look like Little Boy Blue or Little Lord Fauntleroy. For the man you could use small curls ($^1/_{16}$ inch). Men and boys can have very short-looking hair by packing the curls tightly on the head. Section III shows some curly-haired men.

To make sideburns for a man, move some of the curls in front of his ears. Use a straight pin to move the curls around. Use gray curls for sideburns if you want to give him a very distinguished look.

Moustaches and beards, goatees and thick, bushy eyebrows all can be made with curled doll-hair fibers and tiny amounts of glue. You can change the entire image of your doll with only a couple of well-placed curls.

$\mathscr{Chapter}$ 5   Body Building

We now come to the doll's body, from the basic skeleton to the polyester padding.

All dolls need a firm, stable frame, and in this chapter you will learn how to make a wire armature that is sturdy, yet flexible.

Proportion is very important in such small dolls, so I have devised an illustration and guide to making your dolls the right size. No two people are the same, but there are some similarities among everyone.

There are two ways to add hands: one gives an abstract hand shape, the other has separate fingers. There is similarly a simple and a more elaborate way to make feet.

And finally you will literally "round out" your doll with polyester stuffing material, to give some bulk to your men dolls and some curves to your women.

Wire
Armature

The wire armature provides support for the doll and is the basis for the form of the body. The best method for making a sturdy and flexible armature is by twisting together six strands of wire. Any light gauge wire will do, but I strongly recommend the use of "18/3 thermostat wire with casing." You can buy it by the foot at any electrical supply store. The gauge of the wire is 18. In wire sizes, the higher the gauge number, the thinner the wire—20-gauge is thinner than 16-gauge. The "3" indicates three strands of wire twisted together. Each strand of copper wire is coated with a flexible acrylic material, and the strands are encased in an acrylic or soft plastic tube.

Copper wire is best because copper is a very soft, flexible metal. The added protection of acrylic coating makes it exceptionally strong. Steel wire can be used but because it is a harder metal, the wire is stiffer, more brittle, and may break if it is bent back and forth in the same place too many times.

Used in short pieces, 18/3 thermostat wire with casing is sturdy enough to support a small structure. The combination of the soft, pliable properties of copper and the durability of the acrylic coatings makes this wire perfect to use as an armature for a dollhouse doll.

Armature Assembly

1. Cut two 6½-inch pieces of wire, which will give you the six strands you need to make one doll.
2. Remove 3 inches of the casing from each piece by carefully cutting through *only* the casing with your X-acto knife and peeling it away (Fig. 5-1).
3. Keep one of the single strands of exposed wire straight, and bend the other two to opposite sides to form 90° angles (Fig. 5-2). Do this with both pieces of wire.
4. Line the pieces up side by side with the casings touching. While holding the casings (legs) with one hand, use your other hand to twist together the single strands that are sticking straight up (Fig. 5-3). Then, twist together each of the sets of two strands that extend to the sides (arms).

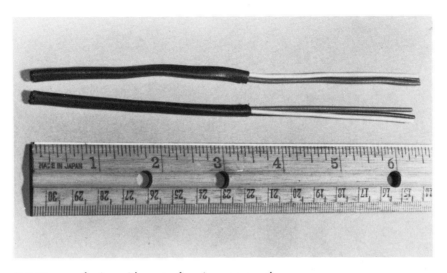

5-1 Pieces of wire with part of casing removed.

5. Fold the twisted center wires down so that only about an inch of twisted wire sticks up above the intersection of all the wires (Fig. 5-4).

5-2 Bend two wires to opposite sides.

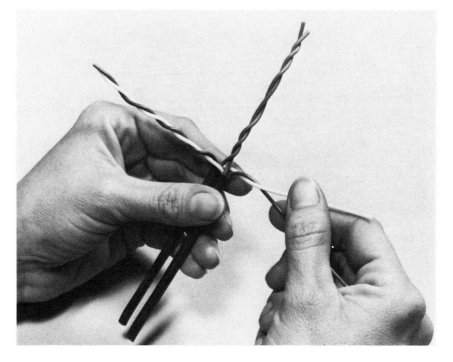

5-3 Twist each pair of wires together.

If the arms seem too long, twist the arm wires tighter. If they are still too long, you can cut them later when you attach the hands. At that time you will pay more attention to proper proportion. If the arms are too short, loosen the twists and pull the wires out, away from the body. If they are still too short, that situation, too, can be corrected later.

Any wire between 16- and 20-gauge can be used by cutting six 6½-inch pieces and dividing the strands into two stacks with three strands in each stack. Then twist each stack of three together about halfway up. These twisted wires would take the place of the wire in casings which form the legs. Then continue as in the instructions above to form the arms and neck.

Although there are many ways to put wires together to make an armature, this design creates the combination of a solid base with flexible limbs. These are qualities you want in a dollhouse doll so it can stand on its own or be posed in

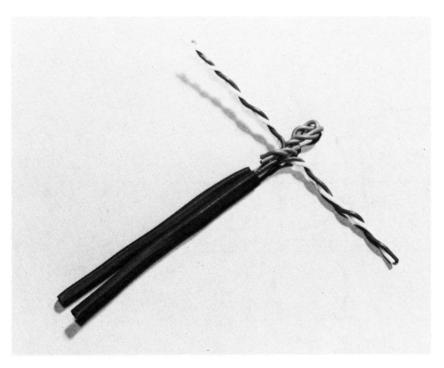

5-4 Fold the top wire over.

miniature scenes. And you need these characteristics because you just *might* want to play with it when you've put it all together!

The height of the body is seven "heads" tall and the various parts of the body can be broken down as follows using the length of the head as the basic measurement:

Rules of Proportion

1 = the head itself
½ = the neck
1½ = from neck to waist
1 = hips
3 = legs
7 heads in all

ARMS. The measurement from fingertip to fingertip is equal to the height of the body. When the arms are straight down, the elbows come to the waist and the hands are slightly

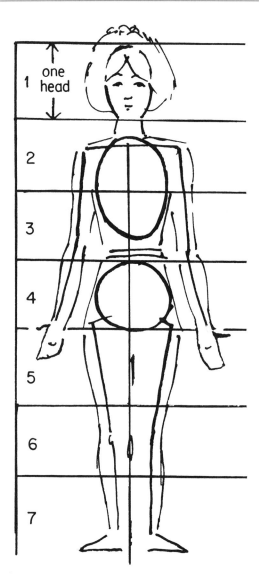

5-5 The body is seven "heads" tall.

below the hips. With arms straight up, the elbows are even with the top of the head.

LEGS. The legs including the feet are three heads long. The knees are halfway between the bottom of the feet and the bottom of the hips (1½ heads).

HANDS. The measurement of the hand from fingertip to wrist is equal to the measurement of the face from hairline to chin.

Breaking the Rules

The dolls you are making are supposed to look as much like real people as possible. People come in many different sizes and shapes; so do dolls! You can bend some of the rules of proportion in order to create a variety of characters.

The heads of dolls representing children are slightly larger in relation to their bodies. For adult dolls you can also make the head a little larger to give it a child-like effect. Exaggerating the size of the face will help to emphasize the character of the doll.

If the waist line is a little bit higher than average, it gives the doll a more graceful effect. But don't raise the waist more than ½ inch unless you want the "fashion doll" look.

Stick to the rules for the length of the arms; if you make them longer or shorter, the doll will look disturbingly out of proportion. Hands that are a little larger than scale are expressive, especially in characters like old farmers or peddlerwomen. Here the size of the hands is indicative of the work they do and contributes to the total image of the character.

Whatever changes you make, always use the rules as a starting point. If changes are necessary to express a doll's character, make sure you don't do anything drastic. Subtle alterations are usually all that's needed.

Hands

There are two types of hands for dolls: hands without fingers and hands with fingers. The first type is obviously easier, and can look very nice if molded carefully. Figure 4-13 in the last chapter showed dolls with the more simple type of hand, although those hands did have separate thumbs.

Undefined Hands

1. Read the previous section to learn how to check the length of the wires for arms and legs. If the wires are too long, cut them. If the wires are too short you will have to compensate by making longer wrists and ankles.

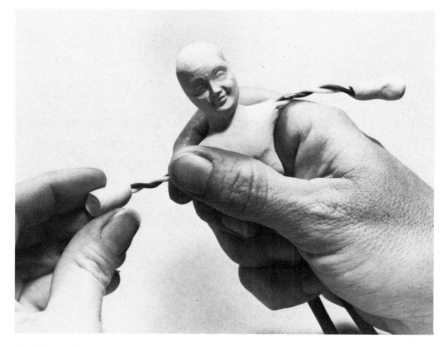

5-6 Press clay cylinders onto arm wires.

2. Make two cylinders of clay about the same size and shape as the eraser on an ordinary lead pencil.

3. Press the wire firmly into the end of a clay cylinder. Make sure it's centered inside the clay.

4. Shape the end of the hand into a slight cone shape and bend the "fingertips" forward slightly to indicate the shape of a hand bent at the knuckles. Only the finger tips will show when the doll is dressed. Smooth any wrinkles in the clay.

5. Check the length of the arms again. Make the appropriate adjustments at the wrists.

6. Squeeze the clay tightly around the wrists to hold it to the wire (Fig. 5-7).

Hands with Fingers

You start these hands with a piece of clay the same size as the eraser from an ordinary lead pencil just as you did in the previous instructions, but this time you do not attach the hand to the wire until you have finished making it.

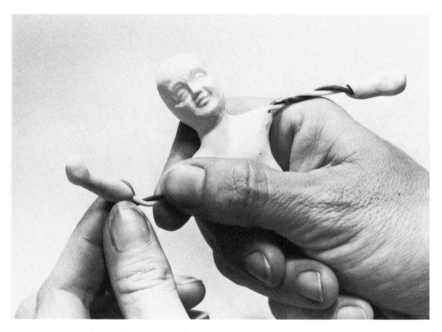

5-7 Squeeze clay tightly around wrist.

1. In the center of the cylinder begin shaping the wrist (Fig. 5-8). This is only so you will have a reference point during the modeling so don't worry if the wrist loses its shape because you will remodel it when you attach it to the wire.

2. Before you start to make the thumb, look at your own; it starts at your wrist. Pull a little bit of clay up from the wrist to make the thumb (Fig. 5-9).

3. Flatten the finger section. Then divide the flattened clay into four sections with your X-acto knife. Cut the sections (fingers) half-way down the hand (Fig. 5-10).

4. Roll each finger between your thumb and index finger to make each one round (Fig. 5-11). If a finger pulls away from the hand gently push it back in place and smooth over the break.

5. Adjust the size of the fingers. The middle finger is the longest, the index and ring fingers are about the same length and of course the "pinkie" is the shortest. If some of your doll's fingers are too long just pinch off the end of the finger and round it off. You can also add

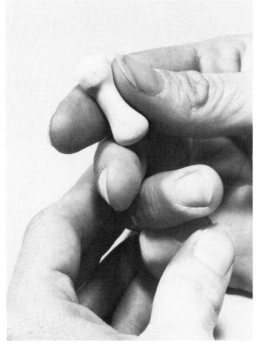

5-8 Shape wrist in center of clay cylinder.

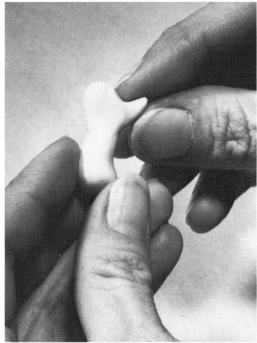

5-9 Pull up a bit of clay for thumb.

clay to lengthen a finger. Press the fingers gently back together so the sides are just touching.

6. Look at your own knuckles to see where the fingers bend. When you bend the clay fingers to close your doll's hand, little clay knuckles will form at the bends in the fingers (Fig. 5-12).

7. Use the head of a straight pin to make impressions that will be fingernails (Fig. 5-13). As you make the impressions you will also be pressing the clay fingers to the rest of the hand, which insures structural stability.

8. With a flat tool, such as a nutpick, press gently on both sides of the largest knuckles (Fig. 5-14). This makes the angle sharp. Remember that even though the outside of the hand is curvey, the structure is based on straight bones which bend at sharp angles.

9. For more detail, make impressions in the back of the hand to indicate the grooves that are between the

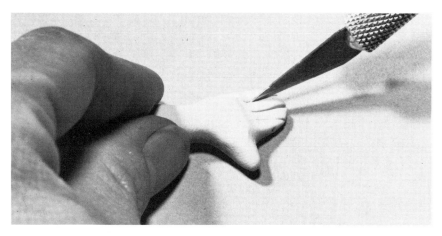

5-10 Cut hand into four sections for fingers.

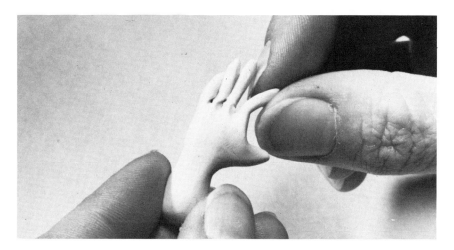

5-11 Gently roll each finger until round.

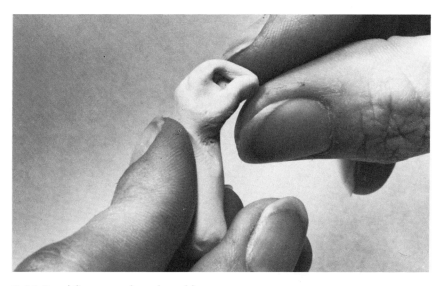

5-12 Bend fingers to form knuckles.

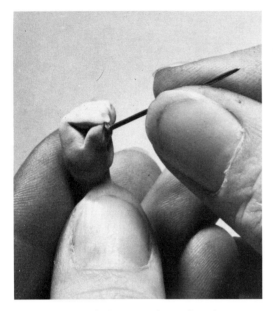

5-13 Press each finger with pin head.

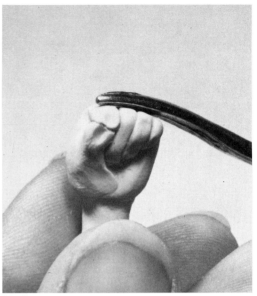

5-14 Flatten fingers to make sharper angles.

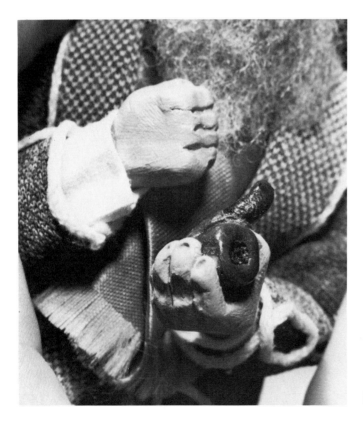

5-15 Finished pair of hands.

tendons. Look at your own hands to see where all the dents and folds are. If you are doing the hands of a young person they would be smoother.

10. Refrigerate for at least 15 minutes so they will be hard enough to hold their shape when you attach them to the wire armature.

11. Press onto the wire and re-form the wrists. (Check to make sure right and left hands are in their proper places.)

Simple Feet

1. Make cylinders for the feet 1½ inches long and a little bit larger in diameter than those you made for the hands.

2. Push the cylinders onto the wires (Fig. 5-16). Push the wires into the ends of the cylinders ¾ inch in and then squeeze the clay tightly around the ankles. Try to keep both cylinders the same size and shape.

3. Lay the doll flat on its back and bend both ends of the cylinders up (Fig. 5-17). This is the beginning of the formation of the shoes.

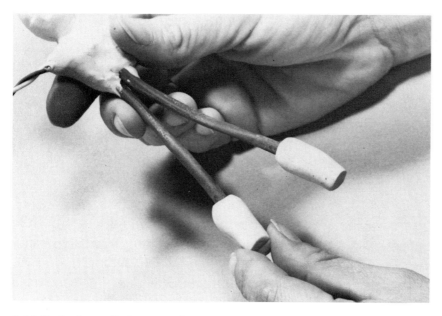

5-16 Push clay cylinders onto leg wires.

5-17 Bend the clay up to form feet.

4. Now stand the doll up on a non-sticky surface, for instance waxed paper or a powdered table top (Fig. 5-18). Push down firmly enough to make the bottoms of the feet flat.
5. Pinch in the arches and gently shape the toes to a slight point (Fig. 5-19).
6. Smooth the wrinkles in the feet and ankles upward. The finished foot should be about ¾ inch long—more or less depending on the size, age, and gender of your character.

Even though the shapes of the hands and feet are quite general and simple, it's difficult to get them to match, especially the feet. However, they are relatively simple to do over again and with a little practice you will find you can make nice even little feet for your doll. Bake the doll in the oven to harden the hands and feet.

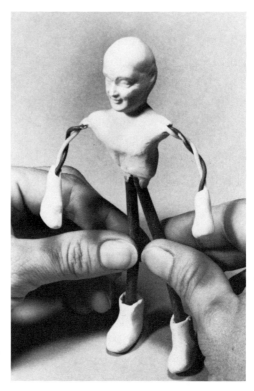

5-18 (Right) Push down firmly to make feet flat.

5-19 (Below) Pinch in the arches and point the toes.

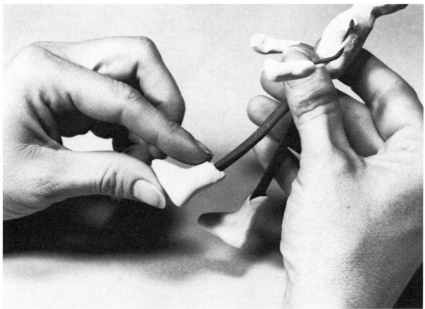

Sculptured Shoes

Contrary to popular opinion, there *are* elves who make tiny shoes. The shoes are beautiful and can be found in most good dollhouse shops and catalogs. Some are leather; some are metal and others plastic. Good plastic shoes and boots are very nice looking; lesser quality plastic can be sanded, painted with gesso and repainted in the color of your choice. These "store-bought" shoes can give your doll a very professional, finished look. Be sure to check the size before buying because some miniature shoes are not in scale and will be too small for your doll.

It is not difficult to make beautiful shoes from clay. Put equal-size cylinders on each foot and bend the cylinders to form a shoe shape. Pinch the toes, heels and ankles for shape and smooth out the wrinkles.

Add more detail to the basic shoe to make your own fancy little shoes. Start a sole by tracing the shape of the bottom of the foot onto a flattened piece of clay. Cut it out with your X-acto knife and press it to the bottom of the foot. This makes a heavier shoe which is quite effective for either men's shoes or sturdy "sensible" shoes for a woman.

Before baking, you can add tiny buckles, seed beads for buttons or any small ornament made from a material that will withstand the heat. Fancy buckles, bows and even shoe strings can be made from clay.

After baking and painting, you can add tiny satin bows to the toes of a lady's slippers. Miniature cloth flowers can add a beautiful touch to shoes.

As you design the shoes, keep the character and the clothing of your doll in mind. Will it be a period doll or a character doll? Decide on the style of the dress and color before you finish the shoes.

Polyester Stuffing Body

The "skinny" wires make a doll look quite comical. During this stage, you will use polyester filling to shape the arms, legs and body. You probably have used this polyester material to make quilts, pillows or soft animals. This time instead of stuffing it you will shape it.

There are many differences in body types, but we will only concern ourselves with the two basic types—man and woman. The ideal shape for a man's body is a V. The ideal body shape for a woman is an hourglass. Of course there are a zillion variations of both of these shapes: fat V's, skinny V's, straight up and down hourglass figures or perfectly round ones. Build the variations to suit your character.

Shaping with polyester stuffing is a wrapping, winding and twisting process. The same principle is used when spinning yarn. The loose fibers of polyester cling to each other when they are being pushed and twisted in the same direction. Of course you won't want them to be twisted together as tightly as yarn. But by loosely twisting the fibers they will hold the shape you give the arms, legs and body.

Shaping the Body

1. Pull off a piece of stuffing about as big as a walnut.
2. Spread it along wire between shoulder and wrist.
3. Wrap it around the wire. It won't stay by itself, so hold your hand around the stuffing-covered wire.
4. Turn the entire doll around and around in your hand—holding the arm loosely enough so the wire

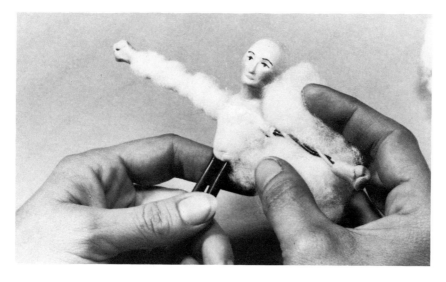

5-20 Spread polyester the length of the arm.

can turn but tightly enough so the fibers in the polyester twist to hold the bulk in place (Fig. 5-21). As you continue turning the doll, add more pressure and the stuffing will fix itself to the wire.

5. Do this with both arms and then the legs, spinning the stuffing tighter at the wrists and ankles (Fig. 5-22).

6. Use a larger piece for the body of the doll. Use the same technique of turning the doll's whole body, but only apply pressure at the waist (Fig. 5-23). When the stuffing is securely attached to the body of the doll, you should have a real hourglass shape!

7. Remove excess stuffing from the top of the doll's back by pulling it out or cutting it off (Fig. 5-24). Leave the bottom intact.

8. In the front, pull the fluffy piece (which would be too much of a pot belly for anyone) between the legs and blend it into the fluff in back to complete the shape of the doll's derriere (Fig. 5-25).

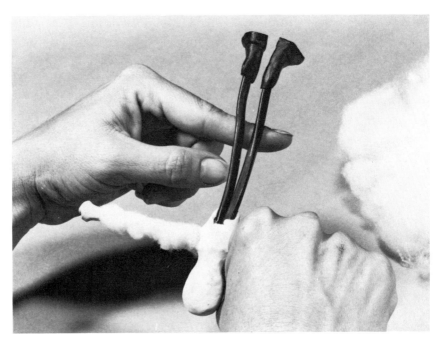

5-21 Turn body to twist polyester.

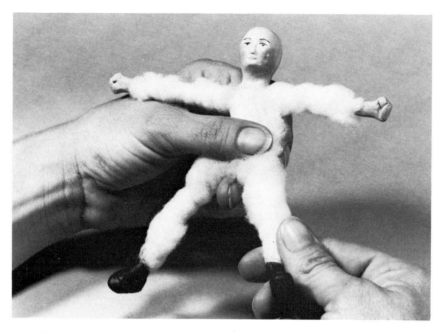

5-22 Cover arms and legs with polyester.

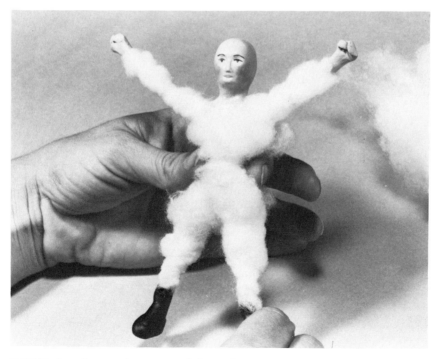

5-23 Twist a larger piece around the waist.

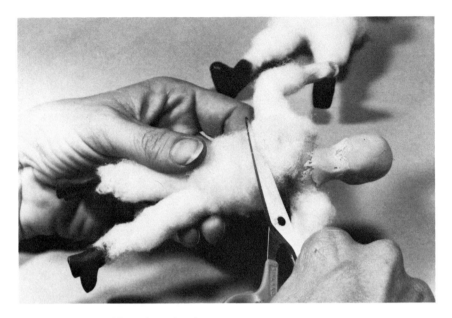

5-24 Cut excess filling from back.

5-25 Pull front piece between legs to back.

9. If you are making a man doll you will, of course, remove the bosom from the front.

10. Use a pinpoint to move the tops of the legs to blend in with the hips (Fig. 5-26). Pull them out and fluff them up more for a woman than for a man. Do the same with the shoulders and fluff them up to give a little more bulk for the man.

11. Wrap ankles and wrists with cloth tape (Fig. 5-27). Tape right onto the top of the clay ankles and wrists to make a secure connection.

12. Make a woman's waist smaller with tape.

All of this stuffing will be covered when you dress your doll. When you glue the clothes in place you can do more shaping by stuffing the clothes if you wish, or pulling the clothes tightly around the body to pack in the stuffing.

5-26 Shape the stuffing into legs and hips.

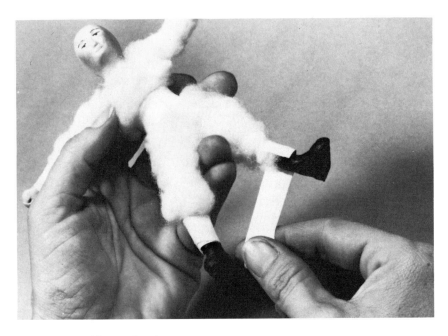

5-27 Tape ankles and wrists.

5-28 Finished male and female dolls.

Section III

ADVANCED COSTUMING

Chapter 6 Period Dolls

Breaking the past up into "periods" is a matter of convenience for historians. Frequently historical periods are defined by the reign of a famous king or queen. Some historical periods, such as the Civil War Period, are just small sections of periods of fashion. From the mid- to late 1800's, fashion periods were divided as follows: Crinoline Period—1840–1869, Bustle Period—1869–1890. Queen Victoria was in power from 1834–1901. Her reign covers both periods, although when most of us think of the bustle, we think "Victorian." We also associate the Civil War Period—1861–1865—with the clothes of the Crinoline Period.

A period doll represents a section of time in history. These dolls can wear nearly exact reproductions of a costume for a specific year. They can also wear abstractions of the costume which give the impression of an exact reproduction by emphasizing the elements of design which characterize the period.

Famous people in history—kings, queens, and other heroes—often inspire dollmakers to make period dolls. Any of the First Ladies are favorite subjects for American dollmakers.

Whether you use a specific person as your example, or a costume of a particular year in history, or the characteristics of the designs of the period, you are making a Period Doll.

Choosing Fabric

The choice of fabric for the dress is an important factor in creating a convincing period costume. As you read fashion history or costume books, you will find that each costume is described in specific fabric types and colors. If you can't use exactly the same type of fabric, use a material that gives the same impression.

If you are lucky enough to have an old dress, once worn by your grandmother and now beyond repair, use the antique fabric. This will add more sentimental value to your doll. The second-hand store is another source for old or antique material. Just make sure the fabric is lightweight; the pattern, if any, must be in miniature.

The pattern or print of the fabric must be in scale. If you choose a print, check or plaid, make sure the pattern is very small. Miniature scale is so tiny that sometimes the smallest-looking prints will be way too big for your doll. So, keep your doll with you when hunting for material. Drape the corner of a fabric piece over her shoulder and you will be able to see immediately if the pattern is the right size.

Make sure that the weight of the material is in scale. If the fabric is too thick, it will bunch up at the seams. Cotton percale is the perfect weight for dresses and shirts. Felt or heavy cotton solid-color denim or kettlecloth are very good for men's pants and jackets. Wool or silk can be used for miniature clothes if the material is not too heavy or too thin.

Choose a fabric that is in character for the period you are reproducing or the personality you are creating. Look in costume history books or old fashion magazines. Translate what you see to miniature scale to achieve the same effect. For instance, in miniature, gray, brown, and dark blue felt look like men's suit material in real-life size.

Make sure the material will work with fabric glue unless your costume will be completely sewn. Most cottons or blends with a high percentage of cotton are excellent. Fabric glue will "reject" most man-made fibers, with the exception of fabrics with nap, such as suede cloth or velvet.

Sewing versus Gluing   The technique that you use for constructing the costume can be sewing, gluing, or a combination of the two. If you want your costume to be totally authentic, you should hand-stitch the entire project. These stitches have to be practically invisible because if the stitches show, they will be too large to be in scale. When sewing hems, your sewing thread should catch only one thread on the outside. Your sewing thread should be very fine, and it should be an exact color match. Sometimes you can unravel some of the dress fabric and use the unraveled strands for sewing hems. All this hand stitching is quite time-consuming and very "picky" work. If you like handwork and have your heart set on a purely authentic period costume, settle into your favorite chair, put on your bifocals and enjoy yourself.

If your goals (and temperament) lean away from hours of minute stitchery, fabric glue is a perfectly legitimate way of connecting two pieces of cloth. Gluing is fast and durable. Some glues require a couple months of drying time, but then the bond is set forever; and the glued seam will last as long as the fabric or longer.

In dressing miniature dolls, it is to your advantage to use a combination of sewing and gluing. Gathering skirts or cuffs is done more easily with needle and thread. When attaching certain accessories, a better job is done with glue. As you decide on which technique to use, consider the type of fabric being used and how it is best handled. For instance, if you are using antique chiffon, you will probably have to sew it because fabric glue will soak through the cloth, discolor it, and make a stiff spot. But when you use felt, you can make a neater, more realistic seam with glue.

Before you begin construction of these period clothes, re-read Chapter 2 to gain a more complete understanding of the basic assembly procedures.

Pantaloons

Underwear

The style of underwear for your doll will vary somewhat depending on the period. You can change the length or fullness of the pantaloons to suit the style of your doll by simply altering the length or width of the pattern. For your Civil War lady, you will want to put ruffled lace trim all the way up each pant leg because the extra lace will add to the effect of the crinoline petticoat. Although wealthy women in the late 1880s also wore many layers of lace on their pantaloons, your Victorian doll's costume should be quite straight and sleek compared to the Civil War lady's dress. In this case you may choose to sacrifice the authentic detail of all that lace on the bloomers, for the all-over effect of the straighter lines of the whole piece.

The following technique for assembling the undergarment is not a new one. It has been used for centuries to attach the arms and legs of china dolls.

1. Measure your doll from her waist to the bottom of her foot and add ¼ inch—this is the "length."
2. Cut two pieces of white muslin—3 inches by the "length."
3. Sew or glue the side seams and the center seam, and cut along pen line (Fig. 6-1).
4. Before turning the bloomers right-side-out, insert one of the doll's feet into each of the pant legs, just enough to cover the doll's ankles.
5. With needle and thread, gather around the bottom of each pant leg and pull the thread tight enough so the gathered pant legs fit snugly around the doll's ankle (Fig. 6-2).
6. Wind the remainder of the thread around and around the doll's ankle, over the gathers to make the connec-

tion very secure. You can also sew or glue a narrow piece of muslin or twill tape over the gathers for added strength.

7. When both legs are gathered and fastened, pull the bloomers up to the waist, turning them right side out. Her feet and ankles will be the only part showing at the bottom.

8. Gather and fasten the waistline of the bloomers just *below* your doll's waistline (Fig. 6-3). Later, when you put the dress on, the waist line of the dress will be *above* the bulky tops of the bloomers and petticoat.

9. The basic bloomer is ready for trimming. Sew or glue tiers of ruffled or flat lace, according to the amount of fullness you want for the doll's petticoats (Fig. 6-4).

Petticoat

1. Measure from your doll's waistline to the bottom of her pantaloons. This is the "length."

2. Cut one white cotton piece this size: the "length" by 6 inches.

3. Connect the back seam (the only seam).

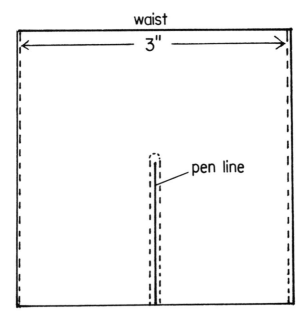

6-1 Sew or glue along dotted lines and then cut along pen line.

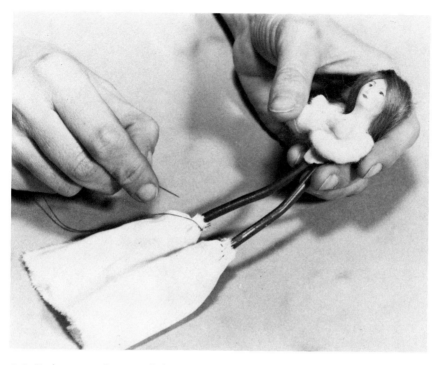

6-2 Gather pantaloons tightly around ankles.

4. Make a ½-inch hem all around the bottom:
   a. For a hoop, use a generous amount of fabric glue for the hem, and inside the hem add a strip of stiff seam binding or interfacing or anything stiff. Even a narrow strip of heavy paper will work. Shape the hoop and let it dry—it will take a while.
   b. For other petticoats, to be worn with less full skirts, hand stitch the hem.
5. Trim with lace. Use tiers of ruffled lace or a single edge of flat lace, depending on the style of dress to be worn over the petticoat.
6. Put the petticoat on your doll, gather the waist and attach it to the bloomers, just below the doll's waist, again to preserve the possibility of a dainty waistline.

Civil War Lady

This dress style is from the Crinoline Period and more specifically from the Civil War Period (early 1860s). This

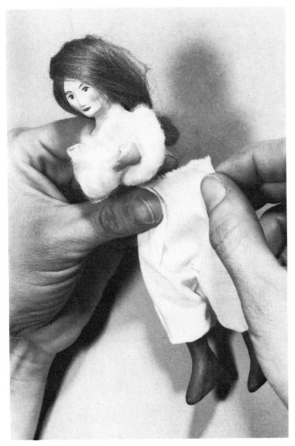

6-3 Pull bloomers up around waist.

6-4 Trim bloomers with lace.

period is named for the many lace petticoats and hooped underskirts which made the full-skirted dresses stand out *so* far from the women's bodies that no one could stand very close. Maybe that was the idea.

These skirts were gathered with much of the fullness in the back, giving the skirt somewhat of a train effect. The sleeves were also very full with a dropped shoulderline. The effect was very soft, flowing and feminine. The bodice was close-fitting and quite tight! The myth of the 18-inch waist was still taken seriously.

The fabrics used were silk, satin, and lightweight woolens. Flounced summer dresses were made from patterned muslin, gauze, or lawn. You can translate this look to miniature by

6-5 A Civil War Lady and Gentleman (actual size).

using light, flowery fabrics for summer dresses and darker colored lightweight cotton or synthetics for winter dresses. Some silk or wool fabrics are appropriate and very pretty, provided they are finely woven and very lightweight.

During the Civil War Period little jewelry was worn; however, gold brooches with semi-precious stones or cameos were popular. Also the black velvet throat band, sometimes worn with a pendant, came back into vogue. The most popular hat was a bonnet, decorated with ribbons or flowers. The shawl continued to be the most popular wrap. Lace gloves, fans and fancy little hankies were all accessories that women of this period liked to carry.

Dress

Lace Neck Inset and Gloves

Use ½-inch ruffled lace trimming to make a lace inset. Glue or sew the gathered edge all the way around her neck; the ruffled edge will cover her chest, shoulders and back. You may cut slits in the outside edge for a better fit.

Lace mitts are glued around the hand and wrist. The outside edge of the lace should start where her fingers would bend. Attach the lace pieces firmly and tightly to the wrist. They can go up the arm as far as your lace goes; the edge will be covered by the sleeve when the costume is completed.

Sleeve Assembly

1. Glue or sew the side seams in the sleeves. Leave them inside out, just as you did for the bloomers.
2. Insert the hand into the sleeve and gather around the wrist. Arrange the gathers so they are evenly distributed around the wrist. Tighten the gathers around the wrist and fasten with glue, sticky tape or a good old-fashioned knot.
3. As you turn the sleeve right-side out, the gathers will stay in place at the wrist and the sleeve will have a blousey effect, leaving only the little lace mitten and hand sticking out of the cuff.

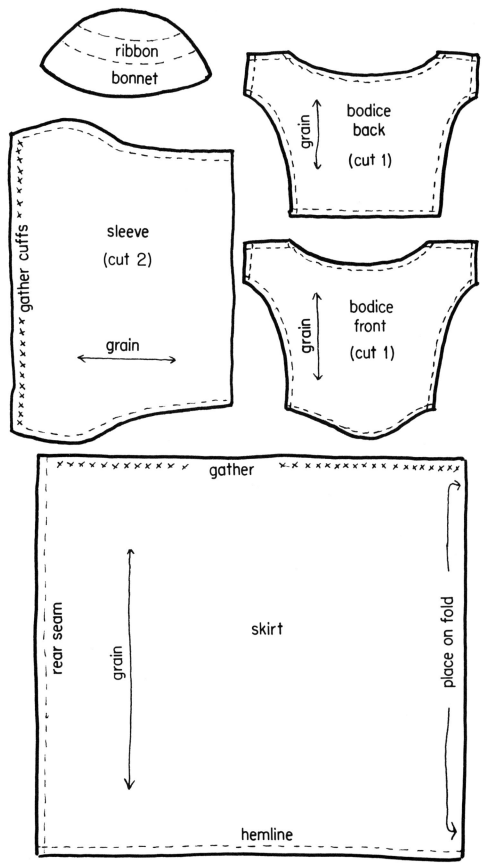

ribbon
bonnet

bodice
back

(cut 1)

grain

sleeve

(cut 2)

gather cuffs

grain

bodice
front

(cut 1)

grain

gather

rear seam

grain

skirt

place on fold

hemline

6-6 Patterns for Civil War Lady's dress.

4. Pull the sleeve up into position at the shoulder. Once again, you must gather around the sleeve, this time at the shoulder. Make the gathers even, front and back, then fasten the sleeve to the shoulder of the doll by gluing or sewing.

Skirt Assembly

1. Sew or glue the back seam of the skirt.
2. Gather around the waist.
3. Put the skirt on the doll and tighten and arrange the gathers so they are evenly placed in the front. Move many of the gathers to the back for extra fullness.
4. Position the waist slightly above the gathered petticoats so your doll will have a tiny waistline.

Bodice

1. Secure all hems by gluing or sewing with tiny invisible stitches. These hems—armholes, neckline, and the bottom of the bodice—are indicated on the pattern piece.
2. Now, working directly on the doll, sew or glue side seams. Make sure the waistline is a very tight fit. Adjust the side seam, making it deeper than indicated on the pattern piece, if necessary to make sure *your* doll has a tiny waist.

The final step in the basic construction of the dress is hemming the skirt. Make sure the slip doesn't show. With all her petticoats this doll is sure to stand on her own without the aid of a doll stand.

Accessories

Accessories are the most important part of creating an illusion in miniature. Here you can give your imagination a real workout: creating lace fans with tiny scraps of lace trim; making soft shawls with fringe out of loosely woven fabric—or do you have an antique, lace hanky? It could be used as a lovely shawl in miniature! And, how will you make that bonnet?

Since jewelry was quite simple during this period, your job as jeweler is made easier. A velvet neckband can be made by sewing a small piece of ⅛-inch black velvet ribbon around your doll's neck. Look through pieces of old costume jewelry for small pieces—parts that would make a good brooch or pendant. You can make a miniature cameo by gluing a tiny piece of white acrylic clay on a black seed bead.

Shawls were the most popular wrap for this period. Make your doll a shawl by cutting a 3-inch-by-3-inch square of soft fabric. Finish the edges of the shawl by adding trim, or fringe the fabric by fraying the edges.

The bonnet was *the* hat for women of the Civil War period. Cut the pattern for the bonnet out of felt, or any stiff material. If you have an old straw hat made with a fine weave, it would make an excellent material for the hat. Trim the edge with lace and decorate with ribbons and tiny flowers. Be sure to try the bonnet on your doll as you are making it, so it will be the right size and the ribbons that tie under the chin will be properly placed.

Civil War Gentleman

The Civil War Gentleman is wearing a costume that is typical of his time. His white shirt has a stand-up collar, with black tie or cravat. His pants are straight and fitted. The most distinguishing characteristic of his costume is his frock coat. These coats were popular through several decades and were made at several different lengths and in varying degrees of fullness—but, *always* cut square at the hemline. The coat this gent wears comes about to the knees and has rather straight and simple lines.

Suits were made in the standard colors for men: black, gray, brown and dark blue. Sometimes trousers were worn in a different color than that of the coat, for less formal occasions.

In this coat, there are no pockets, at least not in the usual places, because coat pockets had not been invented yet! Men of this era did have pockets in the tails of their coats. They stored as many items in their coattails as modern women keep in their pocketbooks. A comb, a handkerchief, money, gloves, even a fan could have been found in the coattail pocket of a Civil War gentleman.

The very ambitious dollmaker could make a lining for the coat, using the coat pattern, and make pockets in the coattails. But, if you do line the coat, use lightweight lining material and hand-stitch, rather than glue, the seams.

The top hat is a must for this costume. It is the accessory appropriate for any elegant gentleman of this period.

Shirt

Use white cotton fabric. Measure the length of the sleeve pattern to make sure it fits your doll. The assembly is the same as all other men's shirts.

Sleeve Assembly

1. Glue or sew the hem on seam line as indicated on pattern.
2. Roll sleeve piece around a large pencil and glue hem over raw edges between "x" and cuffs to form sleeve seams.
3. Bend your doll's arms straight back and slide both sleeves on.
4. Secure front flaps to the doll's body.

Shirt Body

1. Hem (or iron) both armholes on the front and the back.
2. Connect side seams and turn the shirt right-side out.
3. Slide the doll into the shirt—feet first.
4. Sew or glue the shoulder seams in place.
5. Make a single unpressed pleat at the top center of the back of his neck to fit the shirt to your doll.
6. Fold the front on the indicated lines to make the button panel. Secure this fold all the way down.

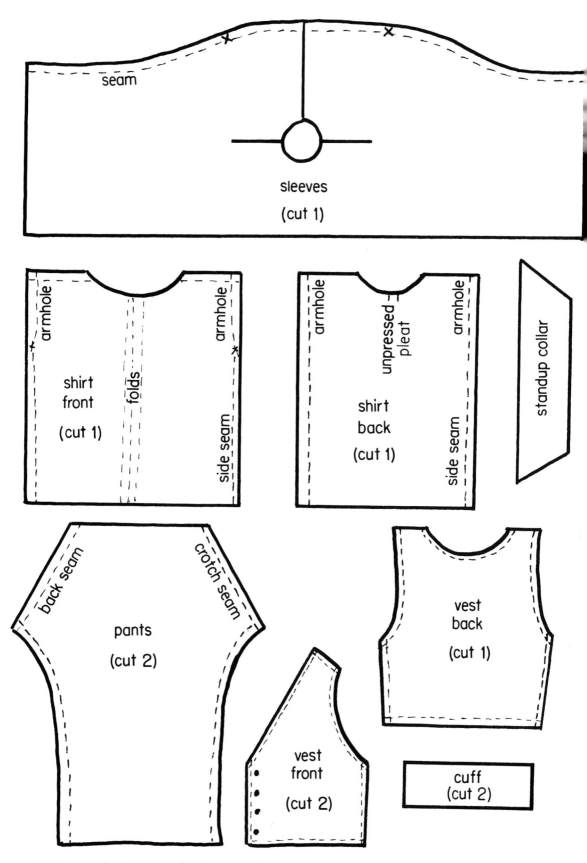

seam

sleeves
(cut 1)

armhole

shirt
front

folds

(cut 1)

side seam

armhole

armhole

shirt
back

unpressed
pleat

(cut 1)

side seam

armhole

standup collar

back seam

crotch seam

pants

(cut 2)

vest
back

(cut 1)

vest
front

(cut 2)

cuff
(cut 2)

6-7 Patterns for Civil War Gentleman's clothes.

Stand-up Collar

1. Measure this collar size by cutting your pattern piece out of paper, then wrap it around your doll's neck, making sure the lower corners meet in the front.
2. Coat a 6-inch-by-1-inch strip of white cotton with fabric glue. Fold in half, lengthwise. Smooth all the air bubbles away and let it dry.
3. Cut out collar and cuffs from this piece (no hems necessary).
4. Glue the collar and the cuffs in place.
5. Gently roll the points of the collar out, away from the doll.

Cravat

If you can find a piece of ⅛-inch black ribbon, you are in luck. Otherwise, use the thinnest, softest, silkiest black seam binding that you can find. Another alternative is cutting a ⅜-inch strip of black lining material, on the bias. Fold the seam binding or lining material into an ⅛-inch strip and iron it, and tie the strip around your doll's neck in a single, simple knot. Wrap the ends around to the back and neatly sew or glue them in place. The back of the collar will be covered by the vest.

Pants

1. Pre-assemble the pants by connecting the front crotch seam.
2. Connect the back crotch seam on the doll—fitting it to his waist.
3. Connect the inside seams, working from the ankles up.

Try to make the pant legs straight and fitted. You may need to poke the stuffing around a little bit as you go along. Check pants assembly in Chapter 2 for more specific directions.

Vest

After you have held up the pattern pieces and adjusted the size, the vest assembly is a fairly straightforward matter.

1. Assemble the front—attach the left and right sides to each other, and add buttons—black seed beads are perfect.
2. Attach the back of the vest to the shirt.
3. Put the front of the vest on the doll, connecting side seams. Cover the top of the pants with the bottom of the vest. And make neat seams at the shoulders.

At this stage you *could* have a finished doll for "inside the house." But don't miss the incredible satisfaction of making the complicated-looking—but easy to put together—frock coat!!

Frock Coat

A good fabric to use for the coat is felt. It is the easiest to handle, especially with the numerous seams on this coat. Also, felt looks like wool in miniature. Some people object to using felt for doll clothes, because it is improperly handled so often. The trick to making felt look rich and the clothes look real is to remove the stiffness and the sheen from the fabric, and the bulky look from the seams.

When the piece of clothing is finished, use an old toothbrush to lightly brush the entire surface of the fabric. Go over the seams, particularly the shoulder seams, so the thick edge of the felt is blended and almost disappears. Then, with a safety razor, lightly remove the fuzz that has come up with the brush. This gives the felt a finish that is more realistic and makes the fabric softer so that it hangs well on the body of the doll.

Sleeve Assembly

1. Connect seams on the sleeves, making them into tubes.
2. Slide them onto the doll's arms.

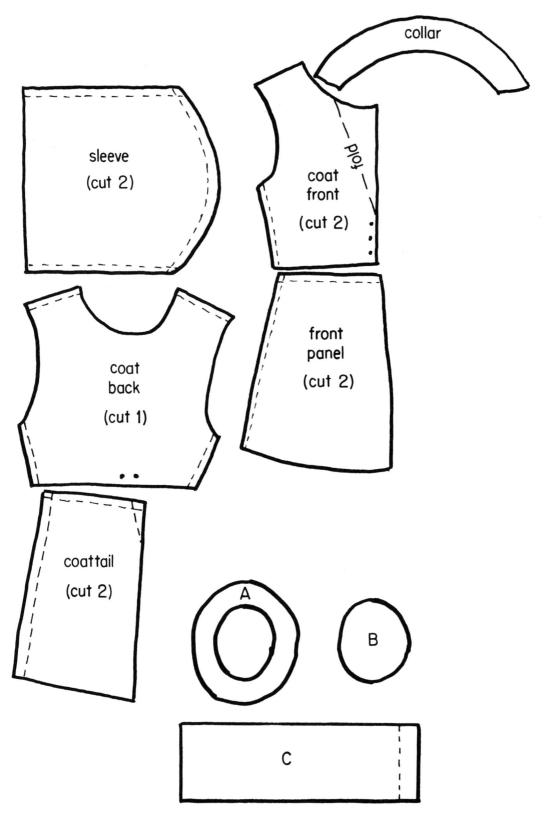

6-8 Patterns for frock coat and top hat.

Coat Assembly

1. Attach front panels to coat fronts.
2. Attach coattails to back, making sure to put the lower edge of the back over the coattails. The coattails will overlap a little in center.
3. Fold the lapels as indicated on pattern.
4. Pin both fronts and back to the doll.
5. Connect shoulder seams.
6. Attach the armholes to the coat sleeves. Be careful not to stitch or glue to the shirt, unless it is your intention that the coat never be taken off.
7. Connect side seams.
8. Attach the coat collar.

Top Hat

After you have cut the felt according to pattern pieces A, B, and C, make a tube out of the B piece. Put a ring of glue on the edge of each end of the tube. Then, simply center the tube on the brim (A). Gently place the crown (C) on top. Let the hat dry thoroughly before trimming the edges to make them as even as you can. Carefully brush the felt with an old toothbrush to level the seams. Glue a narrow black ribbon in place for the hat band. With your acrylic spray coating, spray directly inside the hat! Saturate the hat with spray. Shape it and let it dry.

Victorian Lady

The transition from the Crinoline Period to the Bustle Period was not as abrupt as you might imagine when you look at pictures of typical costumes from each of these periods. At the end of the Crinoline Period, the crinolines were becoming less and less full, and finally the hoop was discarded. The full skirts were gathered to the back and hitched up as a convenience for riding clothes, thus forming a bustle. Eventually bustles became fashionable for day dresses and finally evening gowns, and they stayed in fashion for over twenty years.

The Bustle Period is only part of the Victorian Period, but the bustle seems to be most often identified with the Victorian

6-9 Victorian Lady and Gentleman (actual size).

Period. This design for the woman's dress is from the late 1880's. The line of the skirt is quite sleek, compared to the Civil War dress. The top of the skirt is draped in the front, with an apron. The sleeves are tight, as is the bodice, which stops at the waistline. The dress has a high narrow collar and cuffs, and is trimmed with lace.

The fabrics used for these dresses were cashmere, silk, velvet, and satin. The fabrics were heavier and the effect was more sculptural. In your translation to miniature, heavier fabric, like velvet and some synthetics can be used; however, cotton is heavy enough to hold the shape, drape nicely and still be in scale. It is my favorite because of the variety of colors, finishes and weights available in cotton.

This dress can be made in almost any color (with the exception of strictly modern colors, like orange and aqua). Plaids were popular and so were stripes and floral designs. Very often, this dress style was made with the skirt in a contrasting color. Sometimes combinations of two or three colors will work out beautifully, but other times, because the doll is so small, two-color outfits can make the doll look out of proportion. I recommend sticking with one color for the whole dress, at least on your first one.

There were more "frills" for costumes in this period, and that leaves plenty of room for you to make miniature accessories. Hats were very elaborate, and were worn toward the front of the head. Lace parasols and lace shawls were fashionable. Lace gloves, hankies, and trimming on dresses were all "in."

Dress

The very first step in getting your Victorian Lady dressed is the same as the beginning of the Civil War Lady, putting on the lace collar and cuffs. But, on this doll, use unruffled lace trim. The neckline is high, so only the top edge will show over the collar. Be sure to put the pretty side up!

If you want to give the costume an antique look, dip the lace in a cup of tea—the perfect dye for coloring "antique" lace.

Begin this costume by making the Basic Dress described in Chapter 2. Put the sleeves on as shown, but be sure they are tight. You may need to make deeper seams for a neat fit.

When you fasten the armholes and shoulders, the procedure changes. Follow these steps as you work on the shoulders:

1. Wrap the *front* shoulder tabs back and tuck them *under* the back of the dress.
2. Bring the *back* shoulder tabs *forward*, making sure the armhole seams are even, all the way around on each of the shoulders.
3. Attach the back shoulder tabs to the front of the dress by tacking with a little stitch or some fabric glue. These tabs will be hidden by the vest.

Apron

1. Trim the hemline of the apron with lace or tiny fringe—no wider than ¼ inch. If your trim is wider, attach it to the underside of the hem with only ¼ inch showing.
2. Gather along the top edge of the apron.
3. Fit it to your doll's waist by pulling many of the gathers around to the back on both sides so the piece drapes nicely on the doll.
4. Create a shape with the cloth by pushing the gathers and folds around.

When the apron is evenly shaped and draped, stitch it to the doll's waist. Do not worry about the raw edge at the top; it will be covered.

Overvest

1. Hem all edges of both pieces of the overvest.
2. Connect the left and right sides of the vest at the button panel.
3. Attach the buttons.
4. Glue or sew the overvest directly to the underdress,

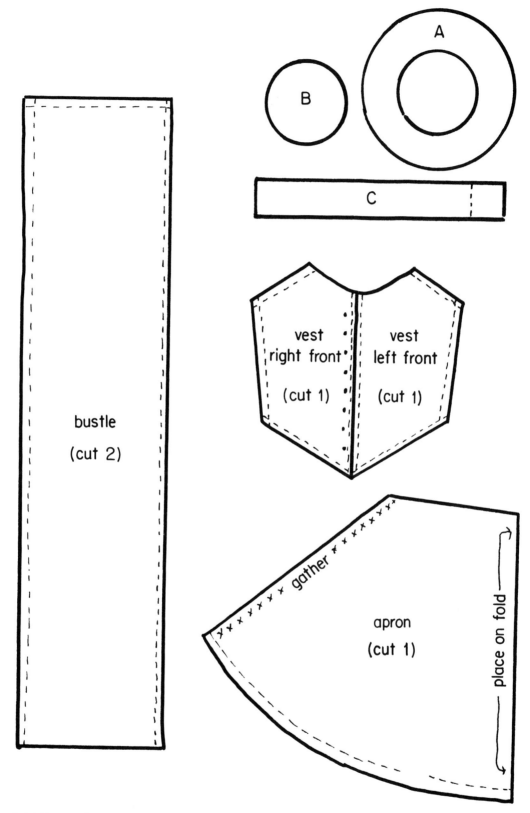

A

B

C

bustle

(cut 2)

vest
right front

(cut 1)

vest
left front

(cut 1)

gather

apron

(cut 1)

place on fold

6-10 Pattern for Victorian Lady's dress.

carefully covering the gathered edges of the top of the apron. Make sure the vest sides cover the side seams of the underdress.

Bustle

The bustle is a separate unit so its construction must be complete before it is attached to the dress.

1. Sew the seams around the edges of the bustle and turn it right-side out.
2. Now tie a big knot—right in the middle—not too tight because the knot *is* the bustle.
3. Pull the two ends together and straight down. Push the fabric around in the knot to make an even shape for the bustle.
4. When it is all finished, attach it to its rightful place covering the gathered top of the apron in the back. All of those extra gathers that were pushed to the rear when you put the apron on will make the bustle stand out even farther.

Hat

The hat is assembled in the same way as the top hat. Make the B piece into a tube, glue both edges and center it on the brim A. Then place the crown on top. Now, the fun of decorating. Let your imagination be your guide. Use feathers, small, cloth flowers, straw flowers, beads, ribbons or anything small.

Victorian Gentleman

The costume for this Victorian Gentleman is a bit less formal than the one for the Civil War Gentleman. His jacket is a "morning" coat. In the late 1800's, it was worn any time of day but, like the bustle worn by his female counterpart, the coat was first designed for riding. The rounded hemline in front allowed much more freedom of movement. It's called a "morning coat" because people did informal things (like riding horses) in the morning.

Because of the less formal style of this coat, the colors can be less sedate. Men were wearing lighter browns, gray-blue, and tweeds. Sometimes the jackets were trimmed in a contrasting color. Like the frock coat, the morning coat was made in several different lengths, but always rounded in the front.

The shapes of men's shirt collars change from year to year—one of the few fast-changing details of fashion for men. This Victorian Gent wears a rounded "turnover" collar which was in style in the late 1800's. It is worn with a knotted tie, but most of the tie is hidden by the high cut of the vest. His trousers have straight legs and no cuffs. This doll has a pocket watch; you can tell by the watch chain that hangs from his vest.

Shirt and Pants

The shirt and pants for the Victorian Gentleman are made in the exact same way as described in Chapter 2 and earlier in this chapter, with these two exceptions:

1. This gentleman's shirt has a rounded turnover collar and a knotted tie.
2. His trousers are a little bit looser (and a bit more comfortable) than those of the Civil War Period.

Vest

The vest is put together in the same way as the Civil War Gent's vest.

1. Hem all the pieces.
2. Assemble the vest on the doll.
3. Using a contrasting color of felt, cut two tiny rectangles to trim the vest pockets. The same color trim will be used for lapels on the Morning Coat.
4. Drape a piece of fine chain from pocket to pocket (*you know there is a watch inside one of those pockets*).
5. Put four buttons—black seed beads—up the front of the vest.

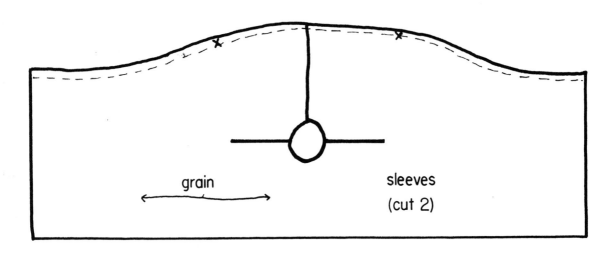

grain

sleeves
(cut 2)

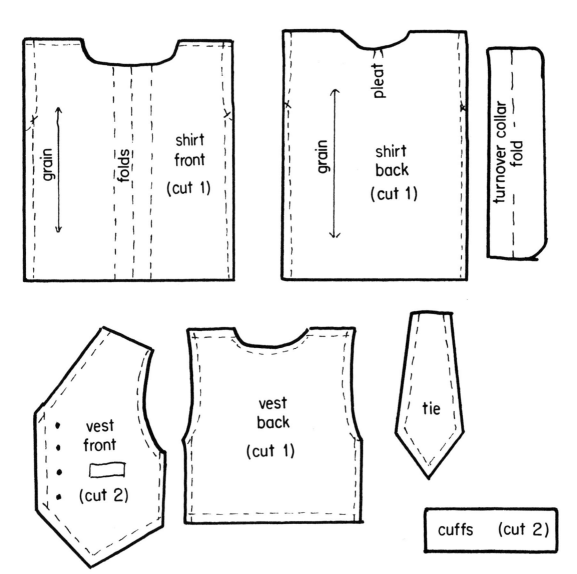

grain

folds

shirt
front

(cut 1)

grain

pleat

shirt
back

(cut 1)

turnover collar
fold

vest
front

(cut 2)

vest
back

(cut 1)

tie

cuffs   (cut 2)

6-11 Patterns for Victorian Gentleman's clothes.

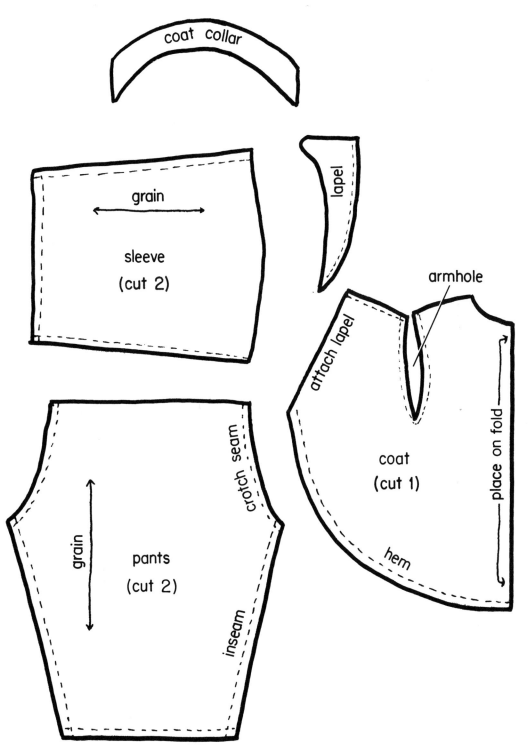

coat collar

grain

sleeve
(cut 2)

lapel

armhole

attach lapel

coat
(cut 1)

place on fold

hem

crotch seam

grain

pants
(cut 2)

inseam

6-12 Pattern for morning coat.

Morning Coat

1. Pre-assemble the coat by hemming the edges indicated, and attaching the lapels.
2. Hem the sleeves and make the seams in the sleeves. Then slide them onto your doll's arms.
3. Put the coat on and connect the armholes to the sleeves.
4. Fasten the shoulder seams.
5. Put the collar on the coat, making sure the edges of the collar meet the tops of the lapels.

Modern Woman

This modern woman is dressed in a skirt and blouse. She wears big boots, a popular fashion accessory for the modern look (but not necessary). Her skirt is a straight skirt or "pegged" skirt, as we called them in the 1950's. The woman's tailored "men's" shirt has been in style (with many variations) for decades. She wears a scarf, tied loosely around her neck. A wide belt with a big buckle cinches her waist. Accessories are the fastest-changing articles in fashion. What this means to you is that you have an infinite number of possibilities for your unique Modern Woman.

If you like the straight skirt, but want your modern woman to be more dressed up, make the skirt and blouse in the same color. Black is always chic. Replace the collar with gold jewelry.

If you have a softer image in mind, use the Basic Dress pattern from Chapter 2. Your choice of material can change the entire character of the dress. The dress length will indicate the year. Hemlines go up and down; the choice is yours. Accessories are very important in creating the image, too. You can make a shirtwaist dress with a button down collar, a Peter Pan collar or no collar at all. A Sailor-boy collar is always cute. Middy dresses began to appear in fashion plates before this century started and have continued to do so periodically throughout the century.

You can make miniature jewelry with chains, beads and parts of old costume jewelry. Belts, sashes, scarves and lace

6-13 A Modern Man and Woman (actual size).

trim can add the little touches that *make* your Modern Woman's outfit.

Blouse

Use the same directions for assembling this blouse as you used for any of the men's shirts. Start with the sleeves, then assemble the bodice, put it on and fasten the shoulders. Attach the collar and cuffs last. There is one major difference in the construction of this garment. Poke some polyester stuffing up under the front of the shirt. Make little tucks or gathers at the waistline to accommodate the extra stuffing. The man's shirt has just become a woman's blouse.

Straight Skirt

The skirt is assembled directly on the doll.

1. Connect the front and back seams.
2. Leave spaces at the hemline for slits.
3. Fit the side seams and shape the skirt as you work, giving the hipline a curved shape. You may need to move the stuffing around to make the Modern Woman look shapely in her straight skirt.

Accessories

I used an old piece of costume jewelry and a scrap of silk seam tape to make this cinch belt. However, there are hundreds or maybe thousands of different ways to make a belt for your doll. Use leather, metal, chain, plastic, cloth or trimming material. Or maybe you would prefer the beltless look.

Here is a wonderful trick for quickly making a scarf. Cut the corner off one of your old scarves and hem the raw edge. Of course, it is easy enough to cut and hem the entire miniature scarf, if you don't have an old one handy.

Modern Man

The modern man, poor guy, has been wearing the same suit for decades. I wonder if it will ever change. Of course, some details change every year or so. On the jackets we have

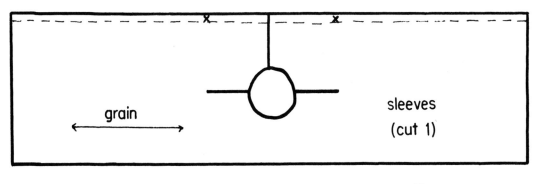

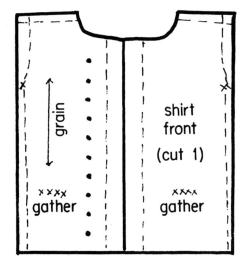

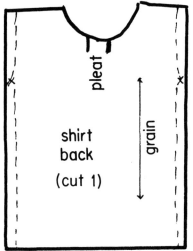

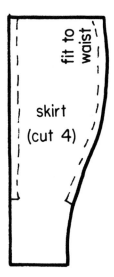

6-14 Patterns for Modern Woman's clothes.

seen different sizes of lapels, varying numbers of buttons, and different lengths and cuts. The pants have had a few small changes, too. Pant cuffs and pleated waists come and go occasionally. The legs get wider and narrower. But the suit retains the same basic structure and so this suit, with minor

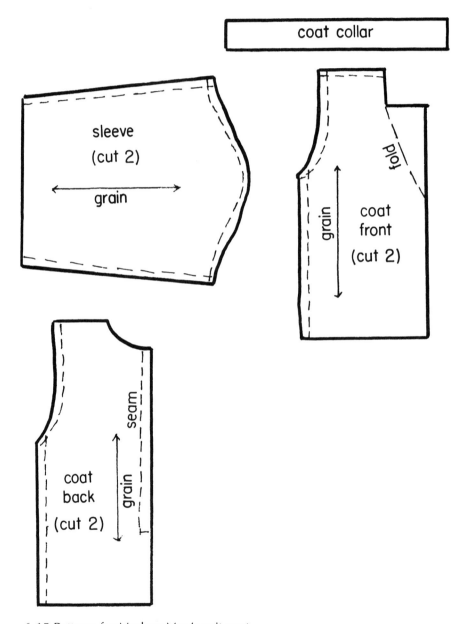

6-15 Patterns for Modern Man's suit coat.

alterations, can fit any year for the Modern Man. This doll wears a charcoal gray suit with the standard shirt and tie. His horn-rimmed glasses are an accessory that maintains the modern look. And for just a little flair, he wears a goatee.

The assembly of his shirt and pants are the same as all of the other men. The shirt could be made in any color or print. The Modern Man can wear a pin stripe or a Hawaiian print. In the Fifties, pink shirts were popular. The white shirt is classic and always in style. On this man, the tie is visible, so hem the edges carefully and fold the top to look like a knot. You can add a tie clip or pin made from bits of old costume jewelry. Add a cuff to his pants if your "year" calls for it.

Suit Coat

Make the coat sleeves first, put in the seams and hem cuffs if necessary. Then, slide them on your doll's arms.

1. Connect the center seam in the back, leaving ¾ inch open at the bottom.
2. Connect front coat pieces to the back of the coat at the side seams.
3. Fold over the lapels and glue or iron them in place.
4. Put the coat on the doll.
5. Attach the armholes to the sleeves.
6. Fit and fasten the shoulder seams.
7. Add the collar, making sure it meets the tops of the lapels.

If you used felt to make this coat, be sure to brush and shave the fabric, as described at the beginning of the chapter.

Chapter 7 **Character Dolls**

Character dolls are my personal favorite. All dolls should be characterful, but in these dolls the character takes over and becomes the most important thing.

Character dolls aren't necessarily pretty, but sometimes they are. They can be period dolls, but usually they are not. They can have any or all of the qualities that other dolls have, but all character dolls must have one special quality: they must tell a story about people. Through clothes, facial structure, setting and accessories, a character doll tells a story about someone we know, or something that has happened in the past, or a situation in everyday life. Sometimes the story is funny and sometimes it's sad, but it is always very dear when it's told in the form of a miniature doll.

Creating a Character

You might wonder why you would have to *find* the character in your doll if you are the one who created it in the first place. These two processes sometimes work simultaneously. When you are working on a doll, planning the style, and concentrating on your dollmaking technique you could be subconsciously creating a character that even you are not aware of until you stop working and take a good long look at it. For example, I made an older gentleman character doll for a scene in a General Store. He was a nice, fatherly type. When my friends saw the finished doll, they said, "Why, it looks just like your father!" And, much to my surprise, it did. Subconsciously, my image of the ideal father was being used to create the character. *After* the creative work was done, I discovered the specific character.

Two of the characteristics that are so universal and basic, that we automatically know what they mean, are age and gender. A mental image is formed immediately when someone says, "an old man, a little girl, a young man, an old woman." These are your first two considerations when designing the body of the doll or its costume.

Facial Expression

If you have mastered face sculpture, you will be able to make faces that are created to express specific characteristics. Women have prettier faces than men, the features are smaller and finer. Like women, young boys and teenagers have high jawlines. Mature men have lower and more pronounced jawlines. Young people have smooth faces; older people have wrinkles.

After you have created a face—male or female, young or old or in-between—take that step a little bit further and show his feelings. You can make your doll happy or sad, worried or fast asleep. Make cry babies or laughing girls and boys. You can also show attitudes with facial expressions such as a haughty dowager with raised eyebrows, pursed lips and nose pointed skyward.

The formation of the features can show what the doll is doing. A musician with puffed cheeks and closed eyes is playing his horn. A doll with his mouth wide open and his head thrown back could be singing a song or delivering a speech.

Clothes

"Clothes make the man" and the women and children, too. This may not be true in real life, but it certainly is true in doll-making. If I make a jolly, old man with a big white beard, he could be any one of a number of characters. But when I put a red velvet suit trimmed with white fur on him, there is no mistaking his identity! Even when the character is not as famous as Santa, the occupation can be shown very emphatically through the costume. A farmer wears overalls; a farmer's daughter wears blue jeans and a gingham blouse (and most likely has pigtails and freckles). A baker is traditionally dressed in white and wears a chef's hat. The old-time butcher wears an apron and a straw hat and straw cuffs to protect his shirt sleeves.

Think of all the characters that derive an identity from the clothes they wear. There are cowboys and Indians, doctors and dance hall girls, sailors, tailors, firemen and businessmen.

Clothing also reflects the lifestyle of your character doll. Country folks wear simple clothes. City "slickers" get all dressed up in the "latest" fashions. This is a good thing to remember for period dolls, too. We usually think of the costumes of the aristocrats, but there are period costumes for the working people, too. So, as you plan your character doll's costume, decide which social circle is appropriate. Will you make an unbleached muslin peasant blouse or a silk brocade gown?

Other countries can be represented by the costumes of character dolls. If you build the image through a common stereotype, the costumes are easy to identify and fun to design. These images immediately come to mind: Eskimos with fur-lined hoods, Scotch men wearing kilts, Dutch women in wooden shoes. But if you want to be accurate, go to the library and do some research! Some of our mental images are far from the true representation of a foreign or ethnic costume.

Another wonderful place to look for inspiration is the land of make-believe. The details of your costumes do not have to be accurate at all. The characters are imaginary; so draw from your own imagination. There are so many characters: Gepetto and Pinnochio, Alice in Wonderland, Cinderella, Sinbad the

Sailor, Goldilocks, Little Red Riding Hood, Santa and his Elves, Snow White and the Seven Dwarfs, to name but a few. You can make magic fairies and gnomes, handsome princes, and wicked witches. The whole world of fantasy is at your fingertips. Costumes for all these characters and more can be made with the use of the basic patterns for dresses, shirts and pants.

Altering Basic Patterns

You can use the basic patterns from Part I and alter them slightly to make many different styles for character dolls. Making the doll fat or skinny is a simple matter of making the

7-1 A puppet-maker from the land of make-believe.

patterns wider or narrower and adding stuffing according to the body size. The pants and shirts for men can be neat and trim or shabby and baggy. The peddler woman in Fig. 7-5 wears the basic dress. With the addition of an apron, shawl and hat, the costume begins to create the character.

Fabrics

The basic dress pattern can be made with almost any fabric. Make it in calico for a pioneer woman. Use a dark color material with a white collar, and the dress becomes a maid's uniform. Dark floral or polka dot is for the old stereotypical image of a grandmother. (The new stereotype is a pants suit!) You can even make the basic dress in brocade or velvet and you have the underdress for a princess.

As you look through fabric shops or through your own scrap bag, you will find fabrics that inspire you to create characters. When you find a piece of dark green velvet, you might think of a Victorian woman in the wintertime. You might pick up a piece of trim with tiny pleats and see it as a skirt for a flapper and you're off to the Roaring 20's.

My mother made all of my dresses when I was a little girl and with the scraps, she made dresses for my favorite doll. If there is a little girl in your life, a matching doll dress is quite a thrill.

Accessories

It's those "little things" that make your character doll or any other dollhouse doll so enchanting. The shopkeeper doll has a pencil behind his ear or a broom in his hand. The little boy holds a toy train. Tiny loaves of bread are lined up in front of the baker. The peddler doll's tray is filled with her wares. The musician's horn, the little girl's apron and the old man's pipe are all accessories that give clues to the identity of the character. The Victorian lady's big, fancy hat, her lace collar and cuffs, her bustle and parasol are her accessories, and all tell who she is.

"The more the merrier" is the rule when it comes to accessories. An abundance of little details makes the most interesting finished piece. This only applies to the art of making miniatures.

There are hundreds of accessories you can make. Most of the materials you use for crafts or sewing can be used for accessories. Salt dough makes perfect bread and other miniature bakery goods. Acrylic clay is good to use for other kinds of food as well as toys, pottery, and flowers. Fabric scraps can be used to make hats, bags, curtains, tablecloths, napkins, towels, and hankies.

There are quite a few different places to look for any of the materials used for making accessories but the first place I

7-2 Accessories are important to a character doll.

always look is around my house. Nothing gives me more pleasure than finding a useless bit of what some people might call "junk" that I have refused to throw away because I might be able to use it for something. When I find a 3-inch piece of rickrack or a broken necklace and say to myself "Ah-ha—exactly what I need," it makes me very happy. It means that I don't have to go out and look for it. I don't have to spend money for it; and momentarily, my inability to throw *anything* away is justified.

So when you are looking for materials for making miniature accessories, take a good look around you. Even if you are not a pack rat, like me, the chances are good you'll find it without even walking out the front door.

There are tiny objects manufactured for purposes other than miniature-making. If you can think "small" as you are shopping or looking around your own home you will see them. A soda pop bottle cap makes a perfect pie pan; a lamp finial is a brass door knob in miniature. The tiny bell at the end of a pull chain can be made into the school marm's bell by gluing a black bead in place for the handle.

Plumbing and hardware stores are ideal places to browse for tiny objects that you can easily convert for use in a dollhouse scene. All of those little copper fittings and gadgets could have a much more interesting future in your tiny scenario. Dime stores and discount department stores are also great places to hunt for potential miniature accessories. Yard sales and garage sales are always good places to look for anything—miniatures included.

MANUFACTURED MINIATURE ACCESSORIES. There are marvelous things made in miniature that are just too impractical to make at home, such as metal and glass pieces, pots and pans, musical instruments and dishes. Printed material is also available in miniature, for example, books that you read with a magnifying glass. You can find posters, playing cards and even tiny greeting cards!

A superior scene is set when you use a mixture of manufactured, hand-crafted and "found" objects for accessories. The three types of miniatures complement each other; each makes the other more believable.

ENVIRONMENT. The background can add so much to the story told by your character doll. Decorate a dollhouse or miniature room to complete the picture. You can even make a corner or small room by wallpapering or painting the inside of the corner of a sturdy cardboard carton. You can create general stores, bakeries, period rooms, or rooms in a modern everyday house.

Setting

SITUATION. Scenes show the character of the doll by having the doll doing something. Pose the dolls in a way that suggests action to tell the story. Instead of lining up four male

7-3 Miniature newspaper and posters help to set this scene.

figures against the wall of your display case, create a situation. Put one in a barberchair and lean all of their heads together; then place some sheet music in one doll's hand and you have a barbershop quartet.

To show the relationship between a mother and daughter, pose the dolls so that the mother is reading a story to the little girl who is snuggled in the mother's lap. Or show the other side of the story. The daughter's hair is being braided and the impatient little girl stares longingly out the window. Look at Norman Rockwell paintings. He had a knack for showing the humor in everyday life situations.

OCCASSIONS. There are many occasions that bring happy memories to all of us. Holidays are particularly good subjects for miniature scenes. Halloween has pumpkins and ghosts. Did you know that miniature jack-o-lanterns that actually light up are available in many miniature stores and catalogs? A Thanksgiving Day dinner scene gives you the opportunity to exercise your skill in food preparation—miniature style. Christmas is a holiday that has many possibilities. Can you imagine 5½-inch Christmas shoppers and carollers? Or Santa and his Elves? Try Santa with a new twist—playing the cello. The traditional Christmas tree would be surrounded by excited children and lots of little toys. Could you knit a stocking that small? A good summer holiday is the Fourth of July. A parade scene could display an interesting mixture of character dolls and period dolls. Birthdays and weddings and Happy New Year parties all make terrific miniature settings for character dolls.

Baker Doll   The Baker is quite a character! His rosy cheeks tell us it is *hot* near the ovens where he bakes his loaves of bread. The costume is traditionally made of white cotton. Use the men's basic patterns for shirt and pants. Add a simple apron of your own design. Crown the baker with a chef's hat and his costume is complete.

Apron

1. Hem all borders of the apron. The bottom border should be below the baker's knees.

7-4 A rosy-cheeked baker with some fresh bread.

2. Attach twill tape apron strings.
3. Put the apron on and tie a bow; trim the apron strings after the bow is in place.

Hat

1. For the headband, cut a long rectangle twice as wide as it will be when finished.
2. Fold the headband in half lengthwise and glue.
3. Measure the head of your doll and glue the headband in a circle to fit.
4. Cut out a circle that is about 2 inches in diameter (or larger if you want a taller crown).
5. Gather around the crown.
6. Fit to the inside of the headband and glue in place.

Bakery Goods

There are many bakery goods you can easily make for your baker doll. They will all look good enough to eat!

Use salt dough for your bread dough. Mix ½-cup white flour, ½-cup salt, ¼-cup water. Knead until the consistency of the salt dough is workable for modeling. Form loaves in the shape of French bread, braided loaves or the standard shaped loaf. A real loaf of bread ranges in size from about 1 foot to 1½ or 2 feet for some French breads. That translates into miniature loaves that are between 1 and 2 inches long. You can make other goodies with salt dough, such as rolls, tarts or coffee rings. Bake your bread at a low temperature—250°— until it is hard and dry. It can take as long as four hours. After the bread is hard, brush the tops of the loaves with egg white and return to the oven for a few minutes at a higher temperature—350°—for golden-brown bread.

On pastries, brush the top with thick white paint or gesso for frosting. Glue a single seed bead on top for a cherry.

You will have to buy a box of Cheerios to make donuts. Several light coatings of acrylic spray will preserve them. Paint them white if you want powdered sugar donuts. Pile them up and glue them together and you will have a stack of donuts.

Cherry pie is a favorite and you can make a miniature version with salt dough for the crust and a bottle cap for the pie pan. Form the bottom crust in the bottle cap. Use red seed beads for pie filling. Make lattice work on top of the beads with tiny strips of bread dough. Bake until the dough is dry and hard. Brush egg white on tip for a golden-brown crust.

To make a cake, use the cap from a small bottle for the base. Paint it with modeling paste, a craft supply which has all the same properties as gesso but is much thicker; in fact it is about the same consistency as cake frosting. Modeling paste can be tinted with acrylic paint. Use a flat modeling tool or the tip of a metal nail-file or nutpick to spread the frosting on the cake.

Use a large button for a plate. For a very fancy effect, cut the center from a paper doily, glue it to the button, center your little cake on the fancy tray and glue it in place.

It is fun to make miniature food because it reminds people of things they really like. Food is associated with many special occasions like birthdays and holidays. See how many kinds of miniature foods you can make for your character dolls. Your advantage in making these miniatures is that you have already made these things in life-size, and believe me, it's much easier to make them in miniature.

The setting for your baker doll can be the kitchen of your Victorian mansion dollhouse or it could be a bakery shop. It can be as simple as a table or counter covered with bakery goods. You could make a butcher, a baker and a candlestick maker and put the three men in a tub.

Flower Peddler Doll

The flower peddler is a study in contrast, between her old, gnarled face and the beautiful flowers. The richness of the color of the flowers emphasizes the faded color of her face and her drab clothes. I used a combination of geometric patterned fabrics for her clothes in opposition to the free flowing forms of the flowers. Flowers symbolize youth, beauty, romantic love and luxury. These things only touch her life in the form of the flowers that she sells.

Clothes

The peddler's dress is made with the Basic Dress pattern. A very plain apron is made using a larger version of the little girl's apron pattern. The shawl is cut from a 4-inch-by-4-inch piece of wool; the frayed edges making the fringe. There are many small touches that could add to the peddler's image. For instance, a hat or a head scarf is easy to make or add a pocket to her apron with a hanky or some money sticking out of it.

7-5 A peddler displays her flowers.

Flowers

All you really need for a flower lady is flowers. Straw flowers are good miniatures; they are easy to find, inexpensive, and available in many colors. Tiny cloth flowers are very pretty and can be found in craft supply stores and stores that sell supplies to milliners. A real find is an old hat with small flowers.

The flowers can be displayed in small boxes, barrels, or cannisters. The holders of the flowers aren't as important as the variation in size and height. When the scene is finished the flowers should be displayed at several levels to make the scene more interesting. The setting for the flower peddler is a city scene.

But don't forget there are country peddlers, too. The old woman selling fruit and vegetables in Fig. 7-2 is a clean-cut, country woman. Her dress is made with the Basic Dress pattern. The fabric is navy blue with white polka dots. Her spotless white collar and cuffs give some insight into her character. Cut a 5-inch length of heavy, wide lace trim and you have a lace shawl. This peddler's tidy dress and shawl, snow white hair and beaming face reflect a totally different life style.

Fruits and Vegetables

Fruit and vegetables are easy to make and they come in handy for enhancing many other miniature scenes, too. They can be used in grocery or general stores as well as fruit baskets or kitchen scenes in a house. Pieces can also be used individually, for example a Halloween pumpkin or one little apple on the teacher's desk to add a subtle touch of humor.

I use acrylic clay for most fruit and vegetables. Apples, oranges, pears and tomatoes are all the round, solid type, so start modeling any of this type fruit or vegetable with a tiny ball of clay. Use a pin head to push in the places for stems. Gently roll oranges and grapefruit on a piece of heavy sandpaper for the right texture.

Leafy vegetables like lettuce are made with strips of light green crêpe paper, dipped in a mixture of white glue and water. Loosely twist the paper around a ball of already baked clay or a large bead. Let it dry and you will have a head of lettuce or cabbage.

You can make the shapes come to life with your paints. Even though the natural colors of the fruit and vegetables are bright, you will still have to tone them down a little bit to make them look real.

Vegetables that grow underground, like carrots and potatoes, can be painted with a brown "wash" (a light watery coat of paint which lets the color underneath show through). The wash will make them look like they just came out of the garden.

The most difficult part of modeling these pieces is getting them small enough. If you measure a real grapefruit you will find that it is about 4 inches in diameter, which translates to ⅓ inch in miniature. An orange is half that size. That's tiny! You have to measure the real pieces of fruit and vegetables to find the correct size in miniature.

The best way to go about making miniature fruit and vegetables is to buy an assortment of the real thing at the grocery store and put it right on your work table. You can measure it and study the shapes and colors while you work and when your work is all finished you will have a nice, wholesome snack waiting for you.

Jazz Musicians

You can tell who these characters in Fig. 7-6 are right away, just by looking at their faces. The horn player's face is shaped for blowing. The piano player looks his part because of his moustache and beard.

They are both dressed in clothes made from the man's patterns in Chapter 2. The horn player is a much "snappier" dresser, so I gave him white pants with wide cuffs and a high waistline. The shirt is pinstriped and the sleeves are rolled— just once. The collar is open to indicate his relaxed attitude. His accessories are a white satin tie, loosened, of course, and thin white suspenders. The horn is the key accessory. It leaves no doubt that he is a very jazzy musician.

The piano player is dressed in jeans and a plaid shirt, which is also a style for the casual mood of a man in his profession. The big accessory that tells the whole story for him is his piano.

The scene is a modern jazz club. The walls are exposed brick. The piano and the tables and chairs were very inexpensive pieces that I painted flat black to blend into the image of a dimly lit nightclub. With the addition of some checkered tablecloths, miniature beer mugs and whiskey bottles and a small audience, the scene is complete.

7-6 Jazz musicians.

Sources of Supply

Boynton and Associates, Clifton House, Clifton, VA 22024
> For a complete list of suppliers of miniatures—building supplies, tools, accessories, furniture and books—send for *The Miniatures Catalog;* 400 pages, illustrated, $14.00.

The Enchanted Dollhouse, Manchester Center, VT 05255
> Accessories and furniture, acrylic clay. General catalog, $1.00; miniatures catalog, $2.00.

My Sister's Shoppe, 1671 Penfield Road, Rochester, NY 14625
> Accessories and furniture. Miniature catalog, $4.00 (refundable with order and coupons included in catalog).

Polyforms Products Company, 9420 West Byron Street, Schiller Park, IL 60176
> Acrylic clays and Sculpey. Free brochure.

Standard Doll Company, 23-83 31st Street, Department DCN778, Long Island City, NY 11105
> Dollmaking supplies and doll parts. Free catalog.

Index